Clinton Fernandes is Professor of International and Political Studies in the Future Operations Research Group at the University of New South Wales. He assesses the threats, risks and opportunities that military forces will face in the future. He co-founded the Indo-Pacific Studies program at UNSW. He is a former intelligence officer in the Australian Army.

'In *Turbulence*, Professor Clinton Fernandes picks up again where he left off from his cogent analysis of "sub-imperial" Australia. This time the focus is on President Trump's geopolitical vision and the frontlines of Europe, the Middle East and China. Australia has its own part to play in all of this; with implications for its own strategic autonomy and sphere of influence.'

Klaus Dodds, Professor of Geopolitics Royal Holloway University of London

'Clinton Fernandes has written a searingly forensic examination of Trump's real agenda. It's a must-read for anyone wanting to understand how radically the US has changed and what it now all means for the rest of us.'

John Lyons, Americas Editor, ABC

'Clinton Fernandes reveals many aspects of today's war-splashed world. Even those Australians who dispute several of his findings will learn much from his pithy book."

Geoffrey Blainey

'This book is a timely attempt to make sense of the unconventional and seemingly chaotic but shrewd "America First" foreign policy of the Trump administration, including to enrich the US, dominate China (including through AUKUS), weaken Europe, and empower Israeli supremacy in the Middle East. Part history, part prediction, the book is an engaging and provocative read by one of Australia's more refreshingly critical foreign policy experts – with lessons for policy makers here and overseas.'

Ben Saul, Challis Chair of International Law at The University of Sydney and the United Nations Special Rapporteur on Human Rights and Counter-Terrorism

'Clinton Fernandes' *Turbulence* is an essential read for anyone concerned with Australia's place and approach in an increasingly conflicted and multipolar world. A timely sequel to his thought-provoking *Subimperial Power*, Fernandes again masterfully examines the dynamics shaping Australia's national security. The book underscores the urgent need for the Australian Government to democratise policy-making by consulting transparently with the Australian people and to align our domestic and international priorities. But this may prove a bridge too far, requiring brave and visionary leadership to unshackle from a constrained and bipartisan understanding of national security. Australia would need to reclaim its commitment to international law and cease its subservience to the United States, including ditching the flawed AUKUS agreement to procure nuclear-powered submarines. *Turbulence* is a vital resource for policy-makers, offering a bold, insightful vision to help guide Australia toward a more independent, secure and prosperous future. Highly recommended.

Major General Michael Smith (retd)

TURBULENCE

AUSTRALIAN FOREIGN POLICY IN THE TRUMP ERA

CLINTON FERNANDES

Melbourne University Publishing acknowledges the traditional owners of the unceded land on which we work, learn and live: the Wurundjeri Woiwurrung peoples of the Kulin Nation. We pay respect to elders and recognise the importance of Indigenous knowledge.

MELBOURNE UNIVERSITY PRESS
An imprint of Melbourne University Publishing Limited
Level 1, 715 Swanston Street, Carlton, Victoria 3053, Australia
mup-contact@unimelb.edu.au
www.mup.com.au

First published 2025

Cover design by Philip Campbell Design
Typeset by Sonya Murphy, Adala Studio

Printed in Australia by McPherson's Printing Group

A catalogue record for this book is available from the National Library of Australia

9780522881325 (paperback)
9780522881332 (ebook)

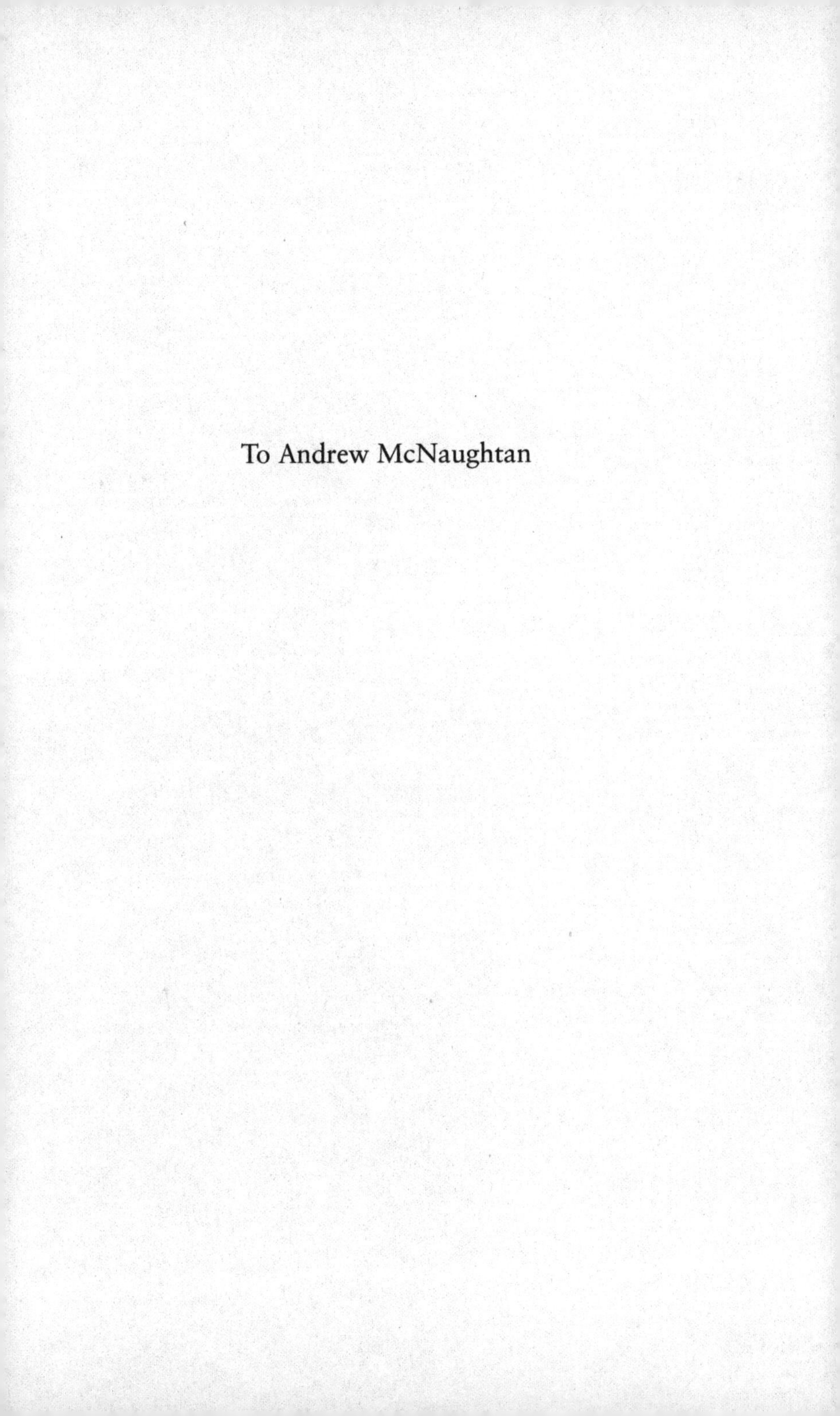

To Andrew McNaughtan

Contents

WHAT IS THE UNITED States trying to achieve in the second Trump administration? What are the geopolitical implications for Australia and the world? These questions are of great interest to many Australians. *Turbulence* tries to explain what US and Australian policy planners are trying to achieve. It was written in November 2024, after the US elections, and in March 2025, in the first weeks of the new administration. The assessment in this book is tentative, not definitive, since the internal planning record will not be available until it is officially declassified many years from now. Nevertheless, an assessment is necessary, to improve the quality of the national conversation.

In the chapters that follow, *Turbulence* explains that Donald Trump's geopolitical goal is to maintain US global primacy against a rising China. He seeks economic control over it. Failing that, his Plan B is economic separation from China. He applies pressure on three geopolitical frontlines: Europe, the Middle East and China. Australia is committed to buying conventionally armed, nuclear-powered submarines in an agreement known as AUKUS – an acronym for Australia, the United Kingdom and the United States. The book contrasts the declared goal of AUKUS with its real goal. The declared goal is to acquire nuclear-powered submarines. The real goal is to demonstrate Australia's relevance to the United States as it tries to preserve US dominance of the region. AUKUS helps Australia join South Korea and Japan as the United States' sentinel states, holding China's naval assets at risk in its own semi-enclosed seas.

'Frontline Europe' shows Trump pushing for a Europe that is subordinate to the United States, economically and politically divided, and geopolitically inconsequential. This has been a consistent goal since his first term; he tried to weaken the European Union (EU) by supporting Brexit and other Eurosceptic forces. He increased cooperation with Poland, the Baltic states and other countries whose leaders were aligned with his geopolitical vision. He remains committed to this goal in his second term. He wants Europe to increase military spending so that the United States can focus on China. He opposes European military autonomy, insisting that Europe remain militarily reliant on the United States for higher end capabilities.

'Frontline Middle East' describes Trump's strategy for a pro-US power centre. Israel's military and technological strength combined with the wealth of energy-rich, authoritarian Arab governments would give Trump veto power over who can access Middle Eastern oil and on what terms. The Abraham Accords, signed in 2020 by Israel, the United Arab Emirates and Bahrain, reflected this strategy in his first term. Trump wants more of the same. Australia's policies towards the Middle East support this geopolitical vision.

'Frontline China' examines perhaps the most important pillar of Trump's geopolitical strategy. Australian foreign and defence policies are most affected by this frontline. A key element is the future of Taiwan, on the edge of mainland China's continental shelf. China cannot reach the western Pacific Ocean without going through the Miyako Strait north of Taiwan or through the Luzon Strait south of Taiwan. Both are within range of US forces in Japan and the Philippines respectively. The Trump administration wants the ability to coerce China in the event of a crisis. Australia's nuclear-powered submarines can support US strategy at this frontline.

'Demonstrating relevance' examines official claims that AUKUS is a nation-building exercise. It shows that AUKUS is just one aspect of a fundamental transformation of Australia's military posture – one that has largely escaped public knowledge although it has been hiding in plain sight. Australia's defence and security establishment has coasted in the slipstream of US military supremacy since the end of World War II. It cooperates almost reflexively when the United States dials up the level of international tension to create a mood of crisis. Short of a serious rethinking, it is likely to persist in this approach. *Turbulence* devotes considerable attention to the United States because of its importance to Australia's external relations.

Trump's shifting of the geopolitical tectonic plates may seem chaotic, but it's not – only his style is, along with what appears to be petty score-settling and other personalised obsessions. *Turbulence* shows that a shrewd geopolitical calculus is at work. But it would be erroneous to attribute all of Trump's strategy to rational, systematic planning. There are non-rational, emotional factors at work, too. As we will see, Trump has been obsessed with tariffs for decades. He does not view international trade as a mutually beneficial interaction between partners but as a means of gaining advantage over rivals. In this worldview, someone is likely to get exploited, and that someone mustn't be him. As *Financial Times* columnist Janan Ganesh suggested, Trump 'has cunning plans ascribed to him by those who find it hard to believe that dogma, caprice and nihilism are factors at the top of politics'.[1] *Turbulence* explores this blend of strategy and personality.

The *New York Times* observed that Australia 'may well be the world's most secretive democracy'. It said that 'even among its peers, Australia stands out'.[2] *Turbulence* is motivated by these concerns. It is an assessment written to inform the public about what the real goals are, not what they ought to be. The latter can emerge from discussions once the former are understood.

1

'We'll get richer if he wins': The Trump agenda at home and abroad

IN MAY 2024, A jury in Manhattan found Donald Trump guilty on thirty-four charges of scheming to illegally influence the 2016 US presidential election. Trump had sought to suppress damaging stories about his personal life, especially those involving allegations of sexual impropriety. He received an unconditional discharge, meaning he did not face fines, prison or any other penalties. As these dramatic events unfolded in public, a jury of a very different kind was meeting in private in Manhattan. At the opulent Pierre Hotel on Fifth Avenue, billionaire Howard Lutnick hosted a fundraiser for major donors to contribute handsomely to Trump's re-election campaign. The event signalled a developing consensus among the ultra-rich in America – a second Trump presidency would benefit them more than anything on offer by the Democratic Party. The key consideration was money.

'We'll get richer if he wins,' as one private equity executive put it.[1] Lutnick, who organised the fundraiser, would become Commerce Secretary in Trump's cabinet.

Less than two weeks after that fundraiser, another private equity mogul, Stephen Schwarzman, announced his support for Trump. Schwarzman, co-founder of investment firm Blackstone Inc., is among the forty richest people in the world, according to the Bloomberg Billionaires Index. Another billionaire, Bill Ackman, founder of investment firm Pershing Square, also declared his support, and others followed. Trump donor Scott Bessent, founder of capital management firm Key Square Group, said that 'Wall Street is definitely swinging in Donald Trump's direction'. Bessent would become Treasury Secretary in Trump's cabinet, which included at least thirteen billionaires with a combined net worth of $460 billion – the 'wealthiest presidential administration in modern history',[2] dwarfing the $118 million combined net worth of President Biden's cabinet. The business press explained why this elite group backed Trump: 'A big reason, in a word: money. Trump has promised to cut taxes for the wealthy and eliminate regulations. President Joe Biden wants the opposite.'[3]

Elections as contests between elite investors

The shift in elite support from Biden to Trump was just the latest episode in a process analysed thirty years ago by political scientist Thomas Ferguson. On the surface, elections appear to be contests between parties for voters. At a more fundamental level, Ferguson demonstrated with detailed evidence in his book, *Golden Rule*, US elections are best understood as contests between elite investors. They form coalitions to fund political parties that advance their agendas against other elite investors' coalitions. What appear to be political conflicts are really the conflicting interests of powerful investor coalitions that select and fund the candidates, heavily influence an administration's programs, and impose constraints on what is permissible.[4]

It should come as no surprise, then, that Elon Musk, the world's wealthiest individual, endorsed Trump, made financial contributions to his campaign, and used his social media platform X to broadcast and amplify pro-Trump messages. Musk once waited in line for six hours to shake Barack Obama's hand. He had quit Trump's business advisory council over his climate change policies in 2017.[5] In similar fashion, financier Marc Andreessen endorsed Trump in 2024. He had backed Hillary Clinton over Donald Trump in 2016 because he disliked Trump's immigration policies. David Sacks, another financier, also switched sides, hosting a fundraiser for Trump in 2024 and urging others to back Trump too. Sacks had supported Hillary Clinton in 2016 and denounced Trump after the riots in Washington DC in January 2021. Trump's promises of tax cuts and looser regulations in finance, cryptocurrency, artificial intelligence and anti-competitive conduct were what really mattered.[6]

Ferguson's work on elections as contests between elite investors applied to the 2016 election as well. When donors realised they had no alternative to Trump being the Republican candidate, they responded in the final weeks of the campaign with 'a vast wave of new money' that caused Hillary Clinton's late-October decline. The money also caused a decline in votes for Democratic candidates for the Senate. Their political fortunes 'unravelled virtually in lock step'. Ferguson's work debunked claims that Russian interference was responsible for Trump's 2016 victory; they could hardly be responsible for the simultaneous 'two declines' that 'very closely track each other'.[7] Trump rewarded his real constituency – the elite investor coalition that backed him – with the *Tax Cuts and Jobs Act 2017*. It increased the national debt by US$1.9 trillion and was forecast to add US$4.6 trillion to the national debt over the next decade.[8] Alan Blinder, the former vice chairman of the US Federal Reserve, denounced its enactment as 'a day of infamy or absurdity, probably both'. The Act was, said Blinder, 'larded with provisions custom-made for the rich and superrich while offering mere crumbs for the middle class'. And 'most of the crumbs disappear' over time while the share accruing to the top 0.1 per cent of taxpayers would rise from 8 per cent in 2018 to 60 per cent in 2027.[9] They blew a large hole in the federal budget – which the second Trump administration will address by slashing spending on government services and imposing public austerity measures.

Trump's agenda in his second term is to serve his real constituency in the business community. One way to serve them is to use the 'defence' industry – a government-funded system that subsidises advanced industrial research and development and ensures profitability by buying the outputs. Members of Trump's coalition have a clear set of economic interests that are more predictable than the diverse, unpredictable utterances of the president himself. They tolerate Trump's personal antics because he retains popular support among his voting base and in Congress, allowing him to implement economic policies that serve their real interests. They went along with 'diversity, equity and inclusion' rhetoric in previous administrations, when they needed it for their 'social licence to operate' – a term that originated twenty years ago in an era of heightened awareness of environmentalism and sustainability, when the mining and extractive industries needed community acceptance.[10] Now that Trump is in power, they have dropped that kind of talk.

Leading figures in this elite investor coalition hold the view that inequality in intelligence and other human capabilities is the natural order of things.[11] Government action to reduce inequality is only a century old. This elite would like to defund government programs that don't cater to their interests.[12] When their priorities sometimes clash with Trump's wishes, a political contest ensues. For example, Trump has long wanted to eliminate the 'carried interest' tax loophole whereby investment fund managers receive a percentage of the funds' profits. The loophole is that these eye-watering earnings are taxed as capital gains (attracting a tax of 20 per cent) rather than as income (which would be taxed at 37 per cent). Trump had denounced this practice in his first presidential campaign, saying:

> I want to save the middle class ... the hedge fund guys didn't build this country. These are guys that shift paper

> around, and they get lucky ... They make a fortune, they pay no tax. It's ridiculous ... The hedge fund guys are getting away with murder. They're making a tremendous amount of money. They have to pay taxes. I want to lower the rates for the middle class. The middle class is the one, they're getting absolutely destroyed.[13]

Trump tried more than two dozen times in his first term to eliminate the carried interest loophole but failed. Gary Cohn, the director of the White House's National Economic Council and a former top executive with Goldman Sachs, explained that there had been intense opposition from lobbyists representing this elite constituency, which 'has a very large presence in the House and the Senate'. He said Mr Trump 'had met his match'.[14] No president this century has been able to fix this disparity and raise the rate, a 'testament to the outsize political strength of the relatively tiny fund-management industry', according to the *Wall Street Journal*'s Eliot Brown.[15] Trump may try again in his second term.

An American sovereigntist

Donald Trump is not an isolationist who wants to withdraw the United States from world affairs. Rather, he is a sovereigntist. Sovereigntists are not anti-interventionists. They are illiberal, reactionary internationalists. They came of age after World War I, when empires began to crumble, trade flows stopped, and new nationalist movements emerged. US politicians, veterans' organisations and Protestant fundamentalists – the American sovereigntists of that era – prevented the United States from joining the League of Nations. They regarded it as a stalking horse for global governance, with unwelcome openings for anti-colonial independence movements, Black internationalists, left-wing political movements and liberal Christians. Sovereigntists opposed US entry into World War II, but they were not isolationists. They 'openly championed the anti-internationalism of the fascists' in Spain and 'accepted – even cheered – the regimes in Nazi Germany and fascist Italy'.[16] They later campaigned against the United Nations and challenged the legitimacy of the International Court of Justice. Many opposed international sanctions on Rhodesia in the 1960s and South Africa in the 1980s. At home, they opposed the *Immigration and Nationality Act 1965*, which loosened immigration for the first time since the 1920s.

Today's sovereigntists aim to weaken non-Western associations that seek a more democratic international order. One such association is BRICS, the inter-governmental association that links Brazil, Russia, India, China and South Africa, and newer members such as Egypt, Ethiopia, Iran and the United Arab Emirates, and potential future members such as Turkey, Vietnam, Thailand, Malaysia and Indonesia. President Trump wants to loosen ties between the core BRICS countries. He offered to sell F-35 stealth fighter aircraft to India to dilute that country's defence ties with Russia. In a similar vein, his overtures to Russia are intended to halt and reverse its deepening relationship with China. He tried to pressure South Africa by cancelling all US aid and other assistance programs and offering resettlement in the United States 'for Afrikaners in South Africa who are victims of unjust racial discrimination'.[17] This last initiative also reflects two other factors – the influence of billionaires with ties to apartheid-era South Africa in Trump's inner circle, and the South African Government's genocide case against Israel at the International Court of Justice.[18]

Under Trump, the United States is at the front of a global wave of illiberal, reactionary political parties in the EU and beyond. They include the Alternative for Germany, the post-fascist Brothers of Italy, the National Rally in France, and the Freedom Party of Austria, which was founded by former Nazi soldiers. They tend to unite on common issues: opposition to certain kinds of immigration, support for 'traditional values', and suspicion of an independent judiciary and liberal media.[19] His administration has made common cause with like-minded sovereigntists, especially in Europe: Viktor Orban of Hungary, Giorgia Meloni of Italy, Marine Le Pen of France and Alice Weidel of Germany. They don't have identical policies, obviously. As the business press says, 'Meloni is a God-and-country conservative; Le Pen a nationalist who believes in state intervention; Weidel a radical libertarian who idealizes Margaret Thatcher'.[20] But they share Trump's suspicion of liberal international organisations.

Trump's demand for control of the Panama Canal as well as Greenland and Canada may seem odd, but he is championing a cause that has existed for a long time. Soon after becoming president in 2025, he requested that a portrait of the eleventh president, James Polk, be moved from the US Capitol to his office in the White House. Polk served for only one term, from 1845 to 1849, but he oversaw the largest expansion of US territory in history. Polk annexed Texas and fought the Mexican–American War, forcing Mexico to cede today's California, Arizona, New Mexico, Nevada, Utah and parts of Colorado and Wyoming in exchange for US$15 million.[21] To avoid fighting on a second front with British Canada, Polk established the United States' northern border at the 49th parallel in 1846. His initial goal had been to annex all the territory up to the southern border of Russian Alaska.

Trump's speech at his inauguration in January 2025 echoed Polk's thirst for territory: 'The United States will once again consider itself a growing nation' that 'expands our territory' and 'carries our flag into new and beautiful horizons'.[22] Trump's wish to annex Greenland and Canada harks back to that era, when US Secretary of State William Seward negotiated the purchase of Alaska from Russia in 1868. Seward wanted to buy Greenland and Iceland, surround Canada, then annex it and create an American Arctic. A century later, when Panama invoked international law and the UN Charter to assert its sovereignty over the Panama Canal, American sovereigntists denounced Presidents Eisenhower, Kennedy, Johnson and Carter for making concessions to it. Trump has revived a long-standing tradition in US geopolitics – an explicitly imperial one.

Imperial since birth

As Niall Ferguson reminds us, the United States was born as an imperial power. Although 'the American people have shown a deep repugnance to both the conquest of distant lands and the assumption of rule over alien peoples', he writes, 'the irony is that there were no more self-confident imperialists than the Founding Fathers themselves'. They saw themselves as empire-builders of enormous scope, despite their fledgling status. George Washington regarded the United States as a 'nascent empire', later an 'infant empire'.[23] Nineteenth-century British naval power thwarted US designs on Canada, as well as its desire to expand south into the Caribbean. But an imperial logic has been present since the beginning of the republic.

Elbridge Colby, a senior Department of Defense official in Trump's first and second terms, explains that the strategic calculations in the early years of the republic were not about isolationism. Discussions about the nature of the US system of government in the 1780s (the Federalist Papers), as well as George Washington's Farewell Address in 1796, were based on a desire to conquer the continent and develop the republic while avoiding entanglement in European wars. Although the United States issued the Monroe Doctrine in 1823 warning European powers not to interfere in the western hemisphere, it lacked the military power to enforce it. But British power on the other side of the Atlantic Ocean kept the Europeans busy. Britain's 'protective shield' allowed the early American republic to 'focus on internal development and expansion while establishing strategic dominance in North America and eventually Central America and the Caribbean'.[24] The 'infant empire' was always intended to be an expansionist one. The Trump administration is well in line with that tradition.

Neo-authoritarianism at home

Trump is part of the American tradition in another, less appreciated way – his authoritarian instincts. Leonard Levy's study of the writings and speeches of the Founding Fathers shows that neither Thomas Jefferson nor Thomas Paine had a problem with criminalising speech that criticised the United States Government. The framers of the renowned First Amendment believed in 'seditious libel' – the mere words of citizens can constitute an assault against the government, and uttering seditious words should be criminal offences. Jefferson objected only to the power of the *national government* to prosecute citizens for verbal crimes. Individual states could and should prosecute citizens for such acts. To think of colonial America 'as a society in which freedom of expression was cherished is an hallucination of sentiment that ignores history', Levy concludes.[25] Only after the Jeffersonians were subjected to repression did they become more supportive of free speech. Seditious libel was finally overturned by the courts more than 150 years later, under the weight of popular pressures and cultural changes in the 1960s.[26]

The cult of personality around Trump is not new either. It is well within the American tradition. A cult of personality around George Washington began at the very start of the Republic 'to cultivate the ideological loyalties of the citizenry', as Lawrence Friedman has shown. Establishment figures 'stressed his flawless essence' and 'consistently asserted that the nation's saviour was without blemish'. 'Mark the perfect man,' they declared. Decades later, he was still described as 'a perfect hero, free from all excess', a man of 'unparalleled perfection', and 'the perfect man' who 'seemed to have been created for the admiration of the world'. He had not always been so regarded; Thomas Paine had called him 'pompous', 'treacherous', and 'a hypocrite'. The editor of one newspaper announced that his retirement would end 'political iniquity' and 'corruption' in the country. But the cult of personality made him out to be 'a demigod-like Founding Father' even though, as Friedman's study showed, 'Western man had rarely declared so much with so little basis in fact'.[27]

Similar cults have been created around later presidents: John F Kennedy, for example,[28] or Ronald Reagan, whose 'spirit seems to stride the country, watching us like a warm and friendly ghost', according to Reagan biographers Martin and Annelise Anderson.[29] Some Australian politicians have photos of Reagan displayed in their Parliament House offices. You might encounter something similar in the media and government buildings in North Korea.

Trump's authoritarian instincts are well suited to the moment. Although he rewards his real constituency, he must also cater to the wider electorate whose votes he and the Republican Party need. Using a familiar playbook, he positioned himself as a defender of traditional America. In January 2016, a year before his first term as president, he gave a speech that was widely reported because he said he 'could stand in the middle of Fifth Avenue and shoot somebody' and 'wouldn't lose any voters'. The media's coverage gave less prominence to something else he said in that speech, delivered at a Christian college in Sioux County, Iowa. He said that 'Christianity is under tremendous siege'. Then, slowly and deliberately, stressing each word, he said, 'We don't exert the power that we should have'. But if he became president, he promised, 'Christianity will have power. If I'm there, you're going to have plenty of power, you don't need anybody else. You're going to have somebody representing you very, very well. Remember that.'[30] They did. Eighty-one per cent of the county voted for him in November 2016. Nationwide, 81 per cent of white evangelical voters did, too.

Trump kept his promise to them, appointing to the US Supreme Court three judges who expanded the place of religion in public life. The court eliminated the constitutional right to abortion in a 6–3 decision on 24 June 2022, which coincided with the day Catholics celebrate the Feast of the Sacred Heart of Jesus. Three days later, the court ruled that a high school football coach had a constitutional right to pray at the 50-yard line, disavowing half a century of precedents that forbade pressuring students to participate in religious activities.[31] Trump also mobilised conservative Christian voters by intensifying his opposition to transgender rights.

His supporters may not want a theocracy, but they would like to see a foundational role for their faith in government. The historic American principle of the separation of church and state is not a core value for them. When Trump left office in January 2021, a survey by the American Enterprise

Institute found that his grassroots supporters were concerned about the disappearance of 'the traditional American way of life'. One in three Americans and a majority (56 per cent) of Republicans believed that 'we may have to use force' to save it. Seventy-nine per cent of Republicans and nearly half of all Americans agreed that the US political system is 'stacked against conservatives and people with traditional values'.[32] They saw Trump as their defender at home.

Minority rule

The Republican Party is supported by a very specific demographic segment, according to public opinion surveys by the Public Religion Research Institute. These are people who self-identify as white, non-Hispanic, Christian, Protestant, and born-again/evangelical. If they check every one of those boxes, they are counted in public opinion surveys as a 'white evangelical Protestant'. Their share of the US population has experienced the most significant drop in affiliation, from 23 per cent of the population in 2006 to 13 per cent in 2023. That is still more than forty-seven million people. They punch well above their weight in elections because they turn out *en masse* to the polls, and they are overwhelmingly clustered into the Republican Party, making up one-third of its voting base. And that gives them a very loud megaphone. Going a little beyond that narrow definition, we get a larger group of 'white Christians'. They were 57 per cent of the US population in 2006 and declined to 41 per cent of the population in 2023. That category now makes up nearly 70 per cent of the

Republican Party's voting base. In the 2024 elections, more than 80 per cent of white evangelical Christians and more than 60 per cent of white Catholics and white mainline/non-evangelical Protestants voted for Trump.[33]

As president for the second time, Donald Trump is not just the leader of the Republican Party; he is also 'the de facto figurehead of conservative American Christianity', according to knowledgeable observers of the contemporary religious moment in America.[34] Many politicians before him have often invoked God or cited the Bible, but Trump is accompanied by Vice President JD Vance, whose strain of Catholicism promotes a traditionalist vision of family life, and Speaker of the House of Representatives Mike Johnson, an evangelical Christian and Southern Baptist. The Southern Baptist Convention is the largest Protestant denomination in the United States. It is often a bellwether for evangelical America. In recent years it has cracked down on women in church leadership, signalling a wider pushback against female power in conservative Christian circles.[35] In addition, a key bloc of Supreme Court judges are Trump nominees. At the highest levels of politics, therefore, all three branches of the United States Government are under the influence of a conservative Christian grouping. All this while President Trump argues that Christians are under siege and need a federal task force to fight anti-Christian bias.

There is the possibility of a major political crisis in the coming years because the US Constitution has a distinctly pro-rural bias. It was framed in the circumstances of the eighteenth century to encourage smaller states to ratify it. The result is that in the twenty-first century, rural voters possess disproportionate electoral strength; states containing as few as 17 per cent of the population can theoretically elect a Senate majority because the least populous states – heavily rural in composition – are over-represented as never before. Democrat voters' tight urban clustering leaves them disadvantaged by the growing unity of rural Americans as a voting bloc. Meanwhile, neither the Episcopal Church, a broadly progressive denomination, nor the historically significant Black church can match the power or influence of the evangelicals.

Ordinary citizens have very little influence on policy when the elite investor class demands something. Robust studies have shown that in the United States, most people's preferences have little or no effect on the decisions of the politicians they elect. Only the people at the very top of the income-wealth scale have their preferences translated regularly into political outcomes. The rest of the population does not have meaningful political representation.[36] The influence of money on US elections leads many younger voters to despair over their political system. A study of US public opinion in May 2024 found that two-thirds of registered voters aged eighteen to thirty years old believed that 'nearly all politicians are corrupt, and make money from their political power'. The pollster, Evan Roth Smith, concluded that 'Young voters do not look at our politics and see any good guys. They see a dying empire led by bad people.'[37]

Cold War 2.0

Trump's geopolitical vision coincides with his elite investors' consensus – they all want the United States, not China, to dominate the global economy of the future. Competition with China is now the organising principle of US economic, foreign and security policies. Trump follows a time-tested plan to advance the cause of the technology moguls: public subsidy, private profit. He has proposed building a missile defence system called 'Golden Dome'. The name comes from Israel's Iron Dome. It harks back to Ronald Reagan's proposal for a space-based missile defence system widely known as 'Star Wars'. It could cost US$100 billion a year for the rest of the decade, and would cover the continental United States, Alaska and Hawaii. To put that figure in perspective, the US Missile Defense Agency has spent about US$200 billion in total since 2002.[38] It doesn't matter that the technology is unproven or that the system can be defeated by adversaries – the point is to get the public to pay for subsidies to the high-tech sector under the cover of national security. This is how the high-tech sector in the United States has always worked, despite the anti-government 'libertarian' rhetoric emanating from it.

The economist Mariana Mazzucato has shown that every technology that makes Apple's iPhone 'smart' was funded by the public, not the private sector. The Internet, wireless systems, global positioning, voice activation and touch-screen displays were all paid for by the American public under the guise of national security. A few examples will suffice here.[39] The magnetic field sensors used in hard disk drives rely on Giant Magneto Resistance (GMR), a quantum mechanical effect observed in thin-film layered structures. GMR was funded by Argonne National Laboratory in the US Department of Energy. It allowed hard drive manufacturers like IBM and Seagate to translate the technology into successful commercial products. Capacitive sensing, another smartphone technology used by Apple, draws on the human body's ability to act as a capacitor and store electric charge. You can use your finger to scroll quickly through the music library on your phone because of capacitive sensing. Multi-touch scrolling came out of Oak Ridge National Laboratory in Tennessee, better known as the site of the Manhattan Project to build the atomic bomb. Apple then acquired this publicly funded research and launched the iPhone.

SIRI, the iPhone's virtual personal assistant, comes out of the taxpayer-funded Stanford Research Institute (SRI) to develop a 'virtual office assistant' to assist military personnel. SRI created the CALO project, the Cognitive Assistant that Learns and Organizes. SRI commercialised the technology by forming 'SIRI' as a venture-backed start-up. Apple acquired SIRI in 2010. Similarly, the US Army funded almost the entirety of the iPhone's liquid-crystal display (LCD) screen. The inventor, Peter Brody, tried to obtain commercial support from Xerox, 3M, IBM, DEC and Compaq. They all refused. Once again, American taxpayers stepped in, giving Brody a multi-million-dollar contract to develop the LCD screen. It is revealing and instructive that Walter Isaacson's biography of Apple's co-founder, Steve Jobs, described as 'the ultimate icon of inventiveness', doesn't mention these core issues even once.[40]

Trump can be expected to continue in this vein. He hailed one of his biggest campaign contributors, Tesla CEO Elon Musk, as 'a super genius. We have to protect our geniuses, we don't have that many of them.'[41] It is a familiar refrain ('a perfect hero', 'a warm and friendly ghost'); meanwhile, Musk and his businesses received at least $38 billion in government contracts, loans, subsidies and tax credits, according to analysis by the *Washington Post*. Tesla would have lost more than US$700 million in 2020, a seventh consecutive year without profits, but government regulatory credits allowed the company to report a profit of US$862 million. Government support, often at critical moments, helped Musk 'seed the growth that has made him the world's richest person'.[42] Trump can be expected to keep these programs going. They will require foreign and defence policies dedicated to creating a strategy of tension, to keep the public subsidies flowing.

Trump's rhetoric and style may be unfamiliar, but his policies are not new; they are reminiscent of earlier episodes in a key US industry – the US aircraft industry immediately after World War II ended. The end of the conflict saw the US aircraft industry producing aircraft at a rate less than 3 per cent of its wartime peak. The business journal *Fortune* warned that 'the aircraft industry today cannot satisfactorily exist in a pure, competitive, unsubsidised, "free-enterprise" economy. It never has been able to. Its huge customer has always been the United States Government, whether in war or in peace.'[43] The problem, as *Fortune* said, was that the aircraft industry feared using the word 'subsidy' because government and industry were 'desperately afraid that someone will come out in open meeting with the word "nationalization"'.[44] The trick was to achieve the 'beneficial effect of a subsidy without the appearance of having taken one'. Air Force Secretary Stuart

Symington advised the Congressional Aviation Policy Board, 'The word to talk was not "subsidy"; the word to talk was "security"'.[45] Accordingly, as Frank Kofsky documented, the United States Government under President Harry S Truman conjured up war scares to justify government intervention.

US commercial aviation benefited from all this. Pan American Airways had been the only US airline offering international flights before World War II. Soon, thanks to these subsidies, there were advanced piston-engine aircraft and new solutions to the problems of navigation and air traffic control. By 1955, more Americans travelled by air than by train. The era of mass commercial air travel had begun.[46]

The semiconductor industry was heavily subsidised too. In its early years, the US military bought the entirety of its output.[47] It was a decades-long public subsidy to the private sector under the cover of national security. Standard works in economics have documented how the Pentagon subsidised IBM's research and development budget, acted as a 'lead user' to guarantee economies of scale, offered vital feedback on how to make improvements, and bought half of IBM's output, 'enabling it to move abroad and flood foreign markets with competitively priced mainframe computers'.[48] Political economist Robert Reich, who worked with the Ford, Carter, Clinton and Obama administrations, noted the amount of money the Pentagon poured into semiconductors, jet engines, composite materials, computers, robots and advanced manufacturing systems during the Reagan administration in the 1980s. He said that 'national defence has served as a convenient pretext for the kind of planning that would be ideologically suspect if undertaken on its own behalf'. He pointed out that Reagan's Star Wars initiative 'promises to be more significant' than the development of the atomic bomb or the Apollo moon program. He explained that its 'real importance' was 'only tangentially related to national defence'. What was the real importance?

> The technology used to create X-ray laser weapons could be applied to super-microscopes; the know-how garnered in designing particle accelerators could be applied to irradiating food products. Spinoffs and applications as yet unimaginable could create whole new generations of telecommunications and computer-related products that could underpin information-processing systems in the next century.[49]

Trump's aggrieved monologues of self-assertion and other elements of his personal style may be unfamiliar, but there is nothing new in principle about a government-funded Golden Dome, travel to Mars, artificial intelligence projects or other welfare initiatives for the technology billionaires. John Kelly, the former Marine Corps general who was Trump's longest-serving chief of staff in his first term, said that Trump 'certainly falls into the general definition of fascist'.[50] But fascism was a serious ideology with an economic program, namely that a powerful state under the leadership of a single ruling party and a powerful leader should command the society, the economy and the corporate bosses. Trump's vision is the opposite of that. His Golden Dome missile defence plans reflect Ferguson's Golden Rule: elite donors from the corporate world invest in a successful election victory and get public subsidies as their payoff.

There are other, more serious costs to Golden Dome: if it were to succeed in defending against missiles, it would destabilise the strategic nuclear balance between the United States and other major nuclear powers such as Russia and China. Nuclear deterrence between these countries rests on nuclear arsenals that can inflict unacceptable damage on each other, preserving a stable balance of mutual vulnerability. A successful missile defence system allows you to hit without being hit. It would let the United States launch its own first strike while stopping an adversary's second strike in retaliation. For this reason, missile defence is really part of an enhanced first-strike system. It would encourage arms racing by other countries to compensate for their vulnerability. It would negate Trump's call for denuclearisation among global powers.[51]

The Pentagon system of subsidising US industry is useful because it excludes the public from the conversation. Ordinary people don't feel confident enough to express their preference about which military project to fund. But social spending has a democratising effect. People feel confident enough to participate in debates about civilian spending priorities. And that is most unwelcome to business and finance leaders and their representatives in the media and the government. As *Businessweek* magazine once observed, there is 'a tremendous difference between welfare pump-priming and military pump-priming'. Spending on welfare and public works 'does alter the economy. It makes new channels of its own. It creates new institutions. It redistributes income. It shifts demand from one industry to another. It changes the whole economic pattern.' But military spending 'doesn't really alter the structure of the economy. It goes through the regular channels. As far as business is concerned, a munitions order from the government is much like an order from a private customer.'[52] That observation is from 1949, at the start of the Cold War, and it retains its cogency.

The Pentagon system of industrial policy today provides a disguised subsidy for high-performance computing systems or 'supercomputers' that bristle with advanced semiconductors. Massive public funding makes the technology workable. The pretext is a familiar one – national security. It is no accident that the fastest supercomputer in the United States is at Lawrence Livermore National Laboratory, where nuclear weapons research funding allows scientists to predict how materials and systems will perform under extreme conditions of temperature and pressure. Another supercomputer at the Air Force Research Laboratory subsidises aerodynamics, propulsion and thermal management through funding for hypersonic weapons research. The Navy contributes by tackling complex hydrodynamic challenges, predicting how new hull shapes and propulsion systems will perform deep underwater. The US Space Force subsidises the future space and near-Earth economy with massive computational power to track satellites, monitor orbital debris and enhance space domain awareness. Another supercomputer at the Pentagon runs complex epidemiological models for biodefence, ensuring a disguised subsidy for drug discovery. The National

Security Agency subsidises the semiconductor industry by buying up billions in computing power, ostensibly to research code-breaking. The National Geospatial-Intelligence Agency spends billions on real-time terrain mapping, precise target detection and other intelligence processes.[53]

These disguised subsidies under the cover of national security require threats, enemies, a global military presence and an atmosphere of tension and patriotism to rally public opinion.

The context for Trump

Trump's first presidency coincided with a time of great financial sickness in the global economy. His campaign emerged from the exhaustion of the neoliberal project at home and abroad. This project replaced the era of regimented capitalism established at Bretton Woods in 1944. That era had sought to deliver full employment and income growth and to make the financial sector the servant of capitalism, not its master. Financiers had been blamed for the Great Depression of 1929 to 1939. Henry Morgenthau, President Franklin D Roosevelt's Treasury Secretary, said that the job of Bretton Woods was to drive 'the usurious money lenders from the temple of international finance'.[54] He insisted on multilateral financial mechanisms to stabilise currency movements and control volatile capital flows, and multilateral development funds to boost productive investment.

Morgenthau explained to the US Congress that his proposals were good for American businesses and households. They would also give other countries enough economic independence – policy space – to let them achieve full employment. What was ultimately at stake, he said, was 'world security and the development of the world's resources for the benefit of all its people'.[55] Regimented capitalism meant first and foremost controlling the financial sector and making it responsive to the needs of the real economy. This wasn't confined to the United States; in the United Kingdom, Hugh Dalton, the first postwar Chancellor of the Exchequer, said he 'must be on the side of the borrowers of money as against the money lenders, on the side of the active producer as against the passive rentier'.[56]

One result of regimented capitalism was the rollback of the financialised capitalism that had brought about the Depression in the interwar years. There was a new social contract centred on economic recovery, regulation of finance, redistribution of income and relief from mass unemployment. The Labor government in Australia published a landmark White Paper, *Full Employment in Australia*, signalling a direct role for government in national development. Despite considerable limitations, the postwar period resulted in a virtuous circle of job creation, productive investment, rising wages and greater productivity.

The era of regimented capitalism ended in the 1970s, during the presidencies of Richard Nixon and Gerald Ford. Carter, Reagan and every president since have operated in an era of neoliberal capitalism, when finance once again became the master, and the rest of the economy the servant. The barriers separating commercial and investment banking were torn down. New, risky financial products were permitted.

Banks were allowed to measure their own risk exposures. The result was uncontrolled cross-border flows of hot money, great wealth for the financial sector, and volatility and risk at levels unprecedented in human history. Monetary policy became the main tool of economic management even as it further damaged an already sick economy.

The global financial crisis of 2008 exposed the hollowness of the neoliberal project. The US Federal Reserve increased the money supply by less than US$1 trillion in the first century of its existence (1913–2008). But, as business journalist Christopher Leonard has shown, the Fed printed US$1.2 trillion between late 2008 and early 2010 – 100 years' worth of money in little over a year. It bought ten-year Treasury bonds – a much bigger deal than it sounds. The Fed had always bought short-term debt because it wanted to control short-term interest rates. But ten-year Treasury bills, or long-term debt, are the equivalent of a savings account. They are a safe place for corporations to store their money. When the Fed bought them up, it reduced the number of safe places to earn a dependable return. This is like a bank taking away your savings account. Savers must experiment with riskier assets or strategies in the hope of higher returns. Economists call this the 'search for yield'.[57]

When the pandemic hit in March 2020, the Federal Reserve pumped another US$2 trillion into the system at first. It kept pumping until its balance sheet increased from US$2.3 trillion to US$8.2 trillion and rising in mid-2021.[58] Showering the country with more money, cheaper loans and easy credit didn't solve the underlying problem of the financial sector being too dominant over the manufacturing and other sectors. It merely kicked the problem down the road. All the new money must now 'search for yield' – investors must look for riskier investments. Financial weakness is part of the environment that brought Trump to power. His elite investor coalition includes several billionaire financiers, and they will want to preserve their power at the apex of the economy. A serious solution would require a return to regimented capitalism, and that is not on Trump's agenda.

Control over or separation from China

Donald Trump emerged from the deterioration of US society after more than forty years of hyper-globalisation. His speech at his first inauguration in January 2017 was a strident denunciation of the past four decades of economic policy: 'the jobs left, and the factories closed'. He described Americans 'trapped in poverty in our inner cities' with 'rusted-out factories scattered like tombstones across the landscape of our nation'. He promised to end the 'American carnage'.[59] The language may have seemed over the top to establishment commentators, but it resonated with many Americans.[60] A year before his election victory, the economists Anne Case and Angus Deaton had documented a phenomenon unknown outside war-torn societies – rising mortality rates among middle-aged, white, non-Hispanic Americans. The increase was due to 'deaths of despair' – suicide, drug and alcohol poisonings, chronic liver diseases and cirrhosis. Those with less education saw the most marked increases in early death rates and addiction.[61] Trump spoke directly to them when he said, 'The forgotten men and women of our country will be forgotten no longer'.

The working-class electoral coalition that brought Trump to office in 2016 was no one-off fluke. Before his victory in 2024, Republican pollster Patrick Ruffini discussed the mounting evidence that a multiracial working-class coalition 'will not only endure but will expand and lend its support to Republicans other than Trump'.[62] It is no accident that Trump began his second presidency by unleashing a barrage of tariffs on the rest of the world. A blend of personality and strategy are at work. He has long been obsessed by tariffs. And he wants to deliver for his new working-class base, capturing a core electoral pillar of the Democratic Party. The tariffs may not ultimately be successful in isolating China, but they show his voting base that he is fighting for them. He wants to construct a new Republican political alignment.

Trump's focus on China stems from a recognition that the global order must be restructured in US interests once again. President Biden recognised this too, telling campaign donors that the United States was 'at an inflection point in history – literally an inflection point in history'.

> [The] decisions we make in the next four or five years are going to determine what the next four or five decades look like ... We were in a post-war period for 50 years where it worked pretty damn well, but that's sort of run out of steam. Sort of run out of steam. It

needs a new – a new world order in a sense, like that was a world order.[63]

Trump is trying to accelerate the pace of the global restructuring. There is less need for US 'soft power' now that the neoliberal project is exhausted and the liberal international order as a global project has collapsed. The Trump agenda at home and abroad follows the Golden Rule. It is primarily the agenda of his elite investor coalition, most notably the representatives of technology, finance, oil, gas and mining interests. It is also, and most prominently, the agenda of the voting base of the modern Republican Party, for whom the separation of church and state are not core values. Resistance to Trump's agenda is likely, at home and abroad. His goal is economic control over China. Failing that, his Plan B is economic separation from China. We now turn to the first frontline, Europe.

2

Frontline Europe

THE RANT, FROM DONALD J Trump, is familiar:

> A lot of people are tired of watching other countries ripping off the United States. They laugh at us behind our backs. They laugh at us because of our own stupidity ... why aren't these countries, these wealthy money machines, paying us for the defence of their freedom and their nations? ... One of the reasons they're so successful is they don't have to worry about defence, because why should they worry about defence when the United States will do it for nothing? ... There are many other countries taking tremendous advantage of this, including NATO. If you look at the payments that we're making to NATO, they're totally disproportionate with everybody else's ... Those countries should be paying us major billions of dollars, and you won't have any

> deficits whatsoever, and then we'll be able to help the poor, and the sick, and the homeless, and the farmers, and everybody else ...[1]

These words were not uttered by President Trump, however, but by Mr Trump in September 1987 in an interview with US television host Larry King. Trump had just spent $94,801 on full-page advertisements in the *Washington Post*, the *New York Times* and the *Boston Globe*, stating, 'There's nothing wrong with America's Foreign Defense Policy that a little backbone can't cure'.[2] He had hired the same public relations executives who created President Ronald Reagan's 'Morning in America' TV advertising in the 1984 presidential campaign. They thought he would run for president in 1988. He was just testing the waters. In the 2000 campaign, when he was briefly a candidate for the Reform Party nomination, he said Japan was 'ripping us big league', Germany 'wants to take over the world economically' and France needed 'to be taught respect'.[3]

Trump's 'Make America Great Again' slogan in 2016 was first used by Ronald Reagan in 1980, 'We Can Make America Great Again'.[4] Trump's advertisements helped him build a national reputation as much more than a real estate developer in a gilded Fifth Avenue tower in Manhattan. The publicity he received in news coverage was worth many times the cost of the advertising. He has a long track record of consistent statements on foreign policy, giving him a certain authenticity now that he utters them with the power of the presidency. He was never enamoured with Europe or NATO;

in his first term, he objected to the disproportionate amounts the United States was spending compared to the Europeans. His administration has made it clear that US priorities are its own region and the Indo-Pacific region. Trump wants a Europe that is economically and politically subordinate to the United States and militarily dependent on it so that he can influence Europe's relations with China.

The deep roots of Trump's European policy

Trump's statements about Europe may seem unfamiliar when compared with recent US presidents, but they have deep roots in US history. The US founders recognised that the shield of British power protected them from European interference in their affairs. For their part, European rulers resented their inability to intrude, and feared the potential threat posed by the American Revolution. They didn't fear an attack by the newborn republic from the other side of the Atlantic Ocean. They feared that ordinary Europeans might regard the American Revolution as an example worth emulating, and republican sentiments of parliamentary democracy might overthrow the established order. Count Metternich, the Austrian Empire's foreign minister and chancellor in the first half of the nineteenth century, wrote to the chancellor of the Russian Empire, condemning the Americans' 'indecent declarations' that 'cast blame and scorn on the institutions of Europe most worthy of respect'. They were 'fostering revolutions wherever they show themselves' and their encouragement gave 'new strength to the apostles of sedition'.[5]

A hundred years later, it was the United States' turn to fear revolution. The Bolshevik coup of 1917, also known as the Russian Revolution, was met with a ferocious reaction by the US Secretary of State, Robert Lansing. He advised President Woodrow Wilson that it represented 'a direct threat at existing social order in all countries'. He wasn't referring to the threat of invasion but the threat of popular forces taking power in their own countries. The Bolsheviks, he said, wanted to overturn 'the present order of things' and were making an appeal 'to the ignorant and mentally deficient, who by their numbers are urged to become masters'. President Wilson agreed. The threat of a good example was serious. In Germany, the government was recognising the soldiers' and workers' councils. In the United States, poorer Americans returning home from Europe expected better working conditions. Wilson remarked to his close aide and medical doctor, Cary T Grayson, that 'the American negro' was most susceptible to such ideas: 'the French people have placed the negro soldier in France on an equality with the white man, and "it has gone to their heads"'. A person who wanted to employ 'a negro laundress' offered to pay her the usual wage in that community. She demanded 'more money than was offered for the reason that "money is as much mine as it is yours"'.[6] Grand visions of foreign policy often conceal such fears in the background.

Democratising sentiments were common after World War I. To crush them, Wilson used wartime powers to crack down on organised labour. David Montgomery's study of the US labour movement describes the violent repression of organised workers and the persistent restrictions on speech and public assembly, long after the Great War had ended. By the time Calvin Coolidge became president (1923–9), 'all but a radicalised handful of workers reported quietly to whatever jobs they managed to hold, discarding their wartime aspirations as the folly of youth'.[7] The United States retained this priority when it helped to liberate Nazi-occupied Europe in World War II. In Italy, for example, the indigenous resistance to fascism had held down six German divisions during the war and liberated most of the country before the British and the Americans arrived.[8] The United States suppressed the anti-fascist resistance and supported fascist collaborators such as King Victor Emmanuel III and Field Marshal Pietro Badoglio. Similar developments occurred in other parts of Europe.[9]

The threat of a good example remains at the core of the United States' counter-revolutionary foreign policy. It reacted harshly when Cuba overthrew its dictatorship in 1959. It understood that Cuban leader Fidel Castro had not demanded the nationalisation of the economy; he wanted representative democracy and social reform. The CIA advised the US Senate in 1959 that Castro was 'not a Communist' and 'not anti-Communist' either. Although the Cuban Communists had the opportunity to organise, they regarded Castro as 'a representative of the bourgeoise' and did 'not consider him a Communist party member or even a pro-Communist'.[10] But the United States recognised the old, familiar problem – the threat of a good example. President John F Kennedy knew that even if Latin America were to 'double its real income in the next thirty years', it would remain 'as poor as it is today

[1961]'. Given 'the influx of the desperately poor into the cities', the 'contrast between luxury and squalor is becoming more visible and explosive than ever'. The US feared 'the spread of the Castro idea of taking matters into one's own hand' in such circumstances.[11] It severed diplomatic relations with Cuba and sponsored an invasion attempt in April 1961. In response, Castro announced his shift to Marxist ideology in a long, rambling speech in December 1961, 'more from pragmatic than from ideological considerations', according to historian Richard Welch.[12]

The threat of a good example explains Trump's instinctive hostility to the BRICS association, and other attempts by developing countries to pursue independent economic integration. Countering that threat remains a central element of US policy planning.

Imperial amnesia

The European Union's self-idealising myths obscure a fundamental truth – US and European elites have a shared interest in a system that privileges elite investor groups. They retain an imperial attitude towards large parts of the developing world. Swedish scholars Peo Hansen and Stefan Jonsson have shown that the EU was founded as an imperialist project. Its self-image today is that European leaders rejected war and embraced peace after World War II. The truth is that they only rejected war against each other, not war against self-determination movements in their colonies.[13] In 1950, French foreign minister Robert Schuman proposed the creation of a

European Coal and Steel Community to make war between France and West Germany unthinkable and impossible. Meanwhile, France was involved in a brutal colonial war in Indochina.[14] A few years later, France, West Germany, the Netherlands, Belgium, Italy and Luxembourg came together in the 1957 Treaty of Rome that established the European Economic Community (EEC), the forerunner to the EU. The EEC included the territories of their colonies, with France conducting vicious colonial warfare against Algeria, and Belgium forcibly holding on to its huge African territories including the Congo. The Netherlands had tried unsuccessfully to re-subjugate the Indonesian people. That history is not part of the EU's manufactured self-image.

European integration would take the competitive element out of European imperialism. It was a cooperative colonial project: Italy and the Netherlands wanted the iron ore in France's African colonies, and all three countries wanted an injection of capital from West Germany, which welcomed the chance to get back into the colonial game. France's industry and its colonies were 'the sumptuous dowry' it brought 'to the wedding basket of Europe'.[15] With considerable insight, Ghana's Kwame Nkrumah likened the Treaty of Rome to the 1884–5 Berlin Conference that had carved up Africa to enrich European empires. Hans Kundnani, formerly at the European Council on Foreign Relations, notes that the contemporary self-image of the EU as a peace project has erased this history. Experts on the EU, including his former colleagues, didn't know about it until he told them.[16]

US postwar planners understood Europe and its imperial mentality. Even before the formation of the European Coal and Steel Community in 1950, US policy favoured 'arrangements whereby a union of Western European nations' would jointly undertake the 'economic development and exploitation' of Africa's colonial and dependent areas. Doing so 'would lend to the idea of Western European union that tangible objective for which everyone has been rather unsuccessfully groping in recent months'.[17] More recently, Europe's benign self-image saw it proclaim that its social market economy and welfare state were a humane alternative to US capitalism. Its top diplomat declared that

> Europe is a garden ... We have built a garden. Everything works. It is the best combination of political freedom, economic prosperity and social cohesion that humankind has been able to build – the three things together. Most of the rest of the world is a jungle, and the jungle could invade the garden.

European diplomats were 'gardeners' who 'have to go to the jungle' otherwise 'the rest of the world will invade us, by different ways and means'. The comments were not unplanned but scripted, and he had employed the jungle metaphor before.[18] The disdain for non-Europeans runs deep in the culture.

Eastern European states that joined the EU after the 1990s often shared this imperial mindset. Although they had benefited from the decolonisation of the Austro-Hungarian and

Russian empires after World War I, they had not shown much solidarity with African and Asian movements demanding independence; rather, during the interwar period, 'intellectuals in Czechoslovakia and Poland demanded that they be given extra-European colonies of their own'.[19] They sought land in West Africa and the Kamchatka Peninsula on the northeast coast of Siberian Russia, arguing that possessing colonies was an integral part of what it meant to be a European nation. They would be welcomed into the EU after the Cold War. But their generous, Communist-era welfare states had to be dismantled as part of the process. The EU limited the extent to which ordinary citizens could influence economic policy. It replaced political contests with rules that could only be challenged in the courts. It created a single European currency on terms preferred by the German central bank, which was insulated from public pressure and focused almost exclusively on preventing inflation.

With economic policy cordoned off, cultural questions took centre stage. One consequence was alarm over immigration and the appointment of a Commissioner for Promoting Our European Way of Life in 2019. The original title was 'Protecting' but it was changed to 'Promoting' to sound less defensive.[20] The EU militarised its sea border with North Africa to keep non-Europeans out, making the Mediterranean Sea the deadliest border in the world. Human Rights Watch said EU migration policy could be summarised in three words: 'Let them die'.[21] It is thus philosophically aligned with Donald Trump's militarisation of America's own southern border with Mexico. European policy planners are upset at Trump's tariffs, economic threats and military posture but basically share his civilisational disdain for the aspirations of the developing countries. Europe cannot match China's outreach to these countries, especially when China says its relationships must go beyond profits to include 'mutual respect, equity and justice'.[22] These countries aren't convinced by European claims that China doesn't really mean this.

Economic subordination

The EU's structure limits its ability to coordinate its economic strategy. Its weakness was most evident during the European debt crisis of 2009–10. The EU recognised the need for overarching, Europe-wide institutions to supervise financial institutions and monitor systemic risk. But the two dozen independent member countries of Europe were unwilling to surrender their sovereignty to a European banking watchdog. No such obstacle confronted Australia or the United States. Both countries enjoy strong central authority. They have a single dominant national language, uniform political and economic institutions from coast to coast, and a federal government. In the United States, the policies of President Barack Obama and the Federal Reserve were implemented across the entire country. These policies resulted in real GDP 16.3 per cent higher in 2011 than it would have been without them, and unemployment almost seven percentage points lower.[23] In Australia, too, economic responses were implemented nationally, and Australia avoided going into recession in 2009.[24] This single national authority – a federal government

– ensured that poorer economies such as South Australia and Tasmania were not treated differently to the rest of Australia. By contrast, the EU recovery model punished poorer economies such as Greece and Spain, imposing austerity on them and creating the conditions for far-right parties to gain popularity in many European countries.

In his first term, Trump tried to weaken the EU by supporting Brexit and other Eurosceptic forces. He faces a less confident Europe in his second term. Germany, the economic powerhouse of Europe, was led by its Chancellor, Angela Merkel, who was very influential in 2016. Now she is out of office and her successors flail about helplessly. Her immediate successor, Olaf Scholz, saw his government fall apart on the same day that Trump won re-election in November 2024. His successor, Friedrich Merz, proposed significant legal changes that would allow him to increase military spending. His economic options are far more limited. The German economy is in recession, its vaunted car manufacturers are in deep trouble due to competition from China's electric vehicles, and its goal of producing one-fifth of the world's semiconductors by 2030 is unravelling. Its vision of a green energy transition faces opposition from voters and the far-right Alternative for Germany party.

In the decade and a half since the global financial crisis, the United States has left the EU in the dust. The two economies were roughly the same size in 2008 but are very different now. Analysts at the European Council on Foreign Relations sounded the alarm when Biden was president, writing that Europe had 'embarked on a process of vassalisation'.[25] Where

Europe's economy had been somewhat larger than America's in 2008 – US$16.2 trillion versus $14.7 trillion, reflecting its larger population (493 million Europeans versus 300 million Americans) – by 2022, the EU and the United Kingdom together had only reached US$19.8 trillion, but the US economy had grown to US$25 trillion. Today, the US economy (population 340 million) is more than 50 per cent larger than the EU's (population 450 million). It is nearly one-third larger than the combined economies of the EU and the United Kingdom (a total of 520 million people). The US dollar was bought or sold in around 88 per cent of global foreign exchange transactions in April 2022 – a share that had not changed much in two decades. By comparison, the euro's share had declined to 31 per cent, down from a peak of 39 per cent in 2010.

The United States is more productive, too; its output per capita is 30 per cent higher than Europe's. American technological dominance over Europe is exemplified by its 'big five' – Alphabet (Google), Amazon, Apple, Meta (Facebook) and Microsoft. These companies dominate Europe's tech landscape with market capitalisations above US$2 trillion, while Europe's five most valuable companies combined do not match the market value of even one US Big Tech company. In 2025, Apple's market value was bigger than the entire German stock market.[26] Not a single corporation founded in Europe in the past fifty years currently has a market value of more than US$100 billion. Europe's most valuable public company is Paris-based luxury goods maker LVMH, not a technology corporation.[27] US advances in machine-learning and artificial intelligence are likely to reinforce US technological dominance over Europe. It is building the high-technology industries of the future.

Of the top fifty technology corporations in the world, only four are European.[28] The seven largest are American. Only two European companies make the top twenty list – ASML, a Dutch manufacturer of photolithography machines used to produce the most advanced computer chips, and SAP, a German software company. When European companies do succeed, they are often acquired by US companies. Microsoft bought Skype in 2011, and Google bought DeepMind in 2014. Europe did not have China's determination to develop its own domestic technology giants. Europe lacks an effective university pipeline needed to feed tech start-ups. Seventeen US universities are in the 2025 *Times Higher Education* ranking of the world's top thirty universities. The UK has five universities in that list. Elsewhere in Europe, there is just one university – ETH Zurich, in Switzerland.[29]

The United States has deep capital markets to raise funds for corporate investment projects. By contrast, Europe has very few of the large pension funds that participate in US capital markets. Paul Achleitner, chair of the global advisory board at Deutsche Bank, says that European investors are 'almost totally dependent on US capital markets. If you want to get anything sizeable done ... you always go back to American investors.'[30] The United States also has plentiful and cheap domestic supplies of energy. Thanks to the shale revolution, it is now the world's biggest producer of oil, with 22 per cent share of the world's total production. Saudi Arabia is a distant second with 11 per cent. Meanwhile, the loss of cheap Russian gas because of sanctions following the Ukraine war has seen soaring energy prices in Europe.

Greater Germany unravelling

The economic centre of gravity in Europe is 'Greater Germany' – an economic zone of 200 million people in interdependent economies. Germany is the centre of the system. Its western flank is Austria, Switzerland, Belgium and the Netherlands. Its eastern flank is the Czech Republic, the Slovak Republic, Hungary, Poland and Slovenia. Germany trades more with the Netherlands than with France, and more with Poland than with Italy.

Greater Germany has historical resonances. After unification in 1871, Germany became a powerful new state in the centre of Europe, replacing what had been nearly forty distinct entities just seven years before. Germany 'eliminated the buffer of "intermediaries" which had so long separated the great powers', as Brendan Simms has shown.[31] It had the most advanced industrial economy, a strong military and an educated workforce. Its foreign policy reflected its nationalism, its idea of a 'German mission' and its central position, or *Mittellage*, between the western and eastern edges of Europe. It wasn't powerful enough to subdue Europe, but it had the ability to defeat any other state. That led to coalitions being built to counter its strength, followed by more German military spending to ensure its security against coalitions, and the competitive spiral continued. What to do about this destabilising dynamic became known as the 'German question'. It took two world wars to answer that question. Postwar Germany lost its aggressive nationalism. But a Greater Germany would retain its economic *Mittellage* – this time between the western and eastern edges of the Eurasian continent.[32] An economically independent Greater Germany may have drifted away from the US-led trans-Atlantic power system.

Italian analyst Marco D'Eramo says that the 'ultimate objective of the German bloc' was 'the creation of a Eurasian continental front with Germany and China as its two extremities, and Russia as an indispensable connector'. This interdependent economic zone aimed to integrate the logistical, productive and energy exporting zones (Russia, Ukraine, Kazakhstan) with exporters of industrial goods (China and Germany).[33] Before the Russian re-invasion of Ukraine in February 2022, four German companies – Mercedes-Benz, Volkswagen, BMW and BASF – were responsible for a third of all European investment in China. Mercedes-Benz sold three times as many cars in China as it did in the United States and counted two Chinese entities as its biggest shareholders.[34] Economic sanctions on Russia effectively put an end to the dream of a common Eurasian space. Instead of a single Eurasian continental front connecting energy, manufacturing and markets, Europe is now reliant on tankers carrying liquefied natural gas from the United States for energy. There are political consequences for this reliance; Europe cannot easily defy the United States.

The status of the gigantic BASF chemical plant in Ludwigshafen, on the river Rhine, is of serious concern. It is the largest single chemical manufacturer in the world, spread out over more than 10 square kilometres. It is the engine of Germany's chemical sector and is reliant on gas, the supply of which is now being curtailed. Its health affects almost every supply chain in Europe. The economies of Poland, the Czech and Slovak Republics and Slovenia have the highest employment shares in vulnerable gas-intensive sectors. Sanctions and other supply-related obstacles have made the price of natural gas about five times higher in Europe than in the United States. It is cheaper to buy ethylene, a building block for plastics, in Texas, and ship it across the Atlantic for further processing in Europe, than to produce it in Europe. Since petrochemicals are intrinsically energy intensive, that is what petrochemical companies say they are doing.[35] The net result is a shrinking of economic activity in Europe, and the loss of jobs. The relative stability and energy affordability in the United States gives it 'a chance to woo big European companies' to leave Europe and move there, the business press reports.[36] Sticking with the current policy jeopardises Germany's economic strategy. It is already resulting in factory closures in Europe.

America's military research and development spending is twelve times larger than Europe's, according to a study on European competitiveness by Mario Draghi, formerly Italy's prime minister as well as the president of the European Central Bank.[37] Draghi proposed investing US$852 billion in innovation; consolidating fragmented industries such as telecoms, energy and finance; creating a single market in services (a bigger sector than manufacturing); deepening debt markets; and upgrading the local defence industry. All well and good, but a single market in services and other proposals are not original ideas; they could have been implemented decades ago had the structure of the EU not been an obstacle.

Ironically, the economic sanctions imposed on Russia may have helped Russian policy planners reimagine their destiny as something more than Germany's resource-rich backwater. Before the February 2022 invasion of Ukraine, foreign corporations had penetrated Russia's economy in almost every sector except the military. Neoliberal ideas were dominant, propelled by Western-oriented oligarchs. Advocates of reindustrialisation under a mixed economic model, such as the Russian Academy of Sciences and the Free Economic Society, lacked influence. Economist James K Galbraith has remarked that breaking the grip of non-Russian actors on Russian economic life would have required 'extra-legal measures reminiscent of a mafia state' such as tariffs, quotas, foreign ownership restrictions, even expulsions of certain enterprises. There 'would have been extremely, and justifiably, harsh' condemnation from the West. While the economic sanctions have imposed costs, Galbraith concludes that they were also 'a gift'; given Russia's large, resource-rich, technically proficient economy, the sanctions have had the effect of enabling 'a strict policy of trade protection, industrial policy, and capital controls' that the Russian Government 'could not plausibly have implemented, even in 2022, on its own initiative'.[38]

Predictions are notoriously difficult, but it may be the case that Russia emerges stronger; it can train a new echelon of technical personnel as it replaces its expended military stocks with better underlying machinery and more advanced technologies.

It remains in control of the key ingredients of success – food, fuel, materials, and scientific and engineering talent.

Europe's regulatory power

The EU has a valuable consumer market of more than 400 million people. From this market comes an important tool of global power – regulatory power. Technology corporations must comply with its regulations that protect citizens' privacy, human rights and consumer rights, or lose access to Europe's $20 trillion market. The regulations can then be exported to or copied by other jurisdictions, forcing technology companies – which are US in origin and in regulatory expectations – to adapt to European standards rather than US ones. Professor Anu Bradford of Columbia Law School has called the EU's ability to export its regulations around the world the 'Brussels Effect'.[39]

Bradford writes that the United States has a 'market-driven regulatory model' that reserves a very minimal role for governments. It privileges the rights of technology companies. China, by contrast, has a 'state-driven regulatory model' that harnesses technology to strengthen government control rather than individual freedom. Its regulatory model is also copied by countries that fear US and EU dominance of the digital economy and want to strengthen their sovereignty over information flows. They are a natural fit with China, which views 'cyber-sovereignty' as part and parcel of its approach to global governance. Sometimes that means insisting on a more central role for the United Nations and its specialised agencies such as the International Telecommunications Union (ITU). Doing so dilutes the power of the United States and its Western allies because of the one-country-one-vote system in the ITU.

The EU approach is less focused on fostering innovation than on regulating and controlling technology. Bradford observes that this approach rests on three core pillars: fundamental rights, democracy and fairness. It wants to rein in the worst excesses of both the US and Chinese 'digital empires' and move them through the power of law towards a more humane future. As such, Europe is primarily a 'regulatory power'.[40] The Brussels Effect means the EU can establish global rules and norms in climate regulations, digital competition, platform accountability and artificial intelligence.[41] And this is precisely what Trump, backed by the technology billionaires who invested in his election campaign, plans to weaken.

Weakening the Brussels Effect

In his first term, Trump called the EU 'a disaster for the United States'. It was a 'foe' that had been created 'to hurt the United States on trade'.[42] He suggested that the EU was an adversary on the same level as China. He demanded that the EU 'take down their barriers' and 'stop charging us massive taxes'. He objected to the EU's regulations and standards, saying that

> We'll make a product, and they'll make a standard that's different than the product, lower or higher. But it's different. So then our product can't come into the EU. They do that all the time. And, frankly, they have

> to start treating our companies better, because they sue all of our companies for billions and billions of dollars. They're picking up all this money from our companies.[43]

He repeated the charge at a cabinet meeting in 2025, saying the EU 'was formed in order to screw the United States. That's the purpose of it, and they've done a good job of it.'[44]

Trump's ambassador to the EU, Gordon Sondland, was blunt about his goals – the EU should drop its regulatory model, which he described as 'protectionist'.[45] He denounced the European Commission as 'out of touch with reality. They are off in a cloud, regulating to their heart's content, and regulating some things that don't even need to be regulated because they haven't even occurred yet, while stifling growth and innovation.' Echoing Trump's long-held views, Sondland said the Europeans were 'enjoying the benefits of a completely disproportionate relationship, and every day that goes by that relationship continues to be disproportionate in their favour. Why would they want to change it?' If we can't fix the problem 'in a voluntary and cooperative fashion, it'll have to be done in other ways'. The main culprit was France:

> The French are heavily involved. They don't seem to care about the German car industry or any other car industry, other than their own. And you know they want to protect agriculture at all costs, even if it completely destabilizes the relationship, and I think they are taking a very parochial view.[46]

Sondland also called for Europe to cut ties with Chinese technology firms such as Huawei if it wanted to enjoy close security, intelligence and technology ties with the United States. A relationship that involved information sharing and intelligence cooperation came with risks, he said, and 'We can't risk being interconnected with someone who has vulnerable technology'.[47] The underpinning feature of all these statements is that the Trump administration wanted to stop Europe adopting policies that helped China's rise.

It is a change from the past, when the United States did not use its security role for one-sided economic advantage. It allowed itself to become the export market for Europe and Japan, helping them recover after World War II. It maintained the international exchange rate structure via the International Monetary Fund and bilateral diplomacy. It ensured a steady flow of capital to borrowers and acted as the lender of last resort during economic crises. It did all this because that was part of its Cold War strategy.[48]

Things are different now. The central front in the struggle for global supremacy is not Europe but China. The priority of US strategy is no longer for European allies to get rich and contribute to the military defence of the continent. Instead, their role is to fit in with US industrial policy, curtail their economic relations with China and help preserve US technological dominance. European security scholar Linde Desmaele argues that the key goal of the first Trump administration was to prevent the EU from being available to China in a way that might support its ambitions vis-à-vis the United States.[49] Accordingly, there are very few purely economic issues; full-spectrum competition with China means the United States will insist on many policy changes that may, on the face of it, have little to do with military power. This time the pressure will be applied against a relatively weaker, less dynamic Europe. Along with economic subordination comes a vision of keeping Europe militarily dependent on the United States.

Blocking European strategic autonomy

There is no contradiction between Trump's insistence that Europe increase its military spending and his goal of keeping Europe dependent on the United States. The two objectives are related. They are also in keeping with the strategy pursued by his predecessors. In 2011, President Obama's Defense Secretary, Robert M Gates, said in his last speech to Europe that it should increase its military spending, warning that, 'The blunt reality is that there will be dwindling appetite and patience in the US Congress, and in the US body politic writ large, to expend increasingly precious funds on behalf of nations that are apparently unwilling to devote the necessary resources' to the military, and 'to be serious and capable partners in their own defence'.[50] He warned that shifting the burden of Europe's defence to the United States was unsustainable. Yet there was no question of encouraging an independent European defence policy. The spending increase had to be part of a NATO plan, which meant that it was subject to US preferences.

The United States wants Europe to spend more on its military but has always opposed Europe's plans to integrate its members' defence forces independently of the United States. That is to say, the United States is opposed to European strategic autonomy. It wants Europe to spend more so that the United States can focus on China, not so that it becomes independent of the United States. Andrew Small of the German Marshall Fund points out that the United States became more interested in controlling Europe once there was a shift towards greater competition with China in non-military matters such as trade, economics and technology. Europe had greater salience in US policy because it was a 'potential force multiplier and a source of additional leverage' in infrastructure finance, investment screening and export controls.[51] The more areas the United States decided to oppose China in, the more relevant Europe became.

When the EU finally responded with a European Defence Fund and a project for military cooperation and development, the United States criticised both initiatives, complaining that they would harm trans-Atlantic cooperation. The proposed fund was taken from the EU budget for research and development. It had US$14.6 billion in planned expenditure over the 2021–7 budget period. The other project was called 'permanent structured cooperation' or PESCO. It involved twenty-five of the twenty-eight EU members working together on cooperative military projects. The United States and the United Kingdom both expressed their opposition, calling the initiatives 'protectionist' and complaining that their defence contractors would be excluded from those projects, which specified that third parties may only 'exceptionally participate'. France and Spain had insisted that intellectual property developed in European defence projects must not be transferred outside the EU, including to European subsidiaries of US companies.

A confrontation ensued at a private meeting in Washington DC in 2019. Michael Murphy, a senior US diplomat with responsibility for Europe and Eurasian affairs, warned EU ambassadors that their initiatives 'could undermine trans-Atlantic security by duplicating NATO efforts and diverting valuable resources' and 'make all of us less safe, Americans included'. He criticised EU states for 'pursuing an industrial policy under the veneer of a security policy', saying that they were trying to exclude participation and competition by NATO members that were not part of the EU, such as Canada, Norway, the United Kingdom after Brexit and the United States itself.[52] The US ambassador to NATO, Kay Bailey Hutchison, also warned Europe against what she called 'a protectionist vehicle' for the EU, saying, 'we're going to watch carefully because if that becomes the case, then it could splinter the strong security alliance that we have'. Hutchison specifically objected to the idea that nations outside PESCO could be cut off from sales to European nations: 'We want the Europeans to have capabilities and strength, but not to fence off American products ... Norwegian products ... or UK products'.[53] Sondland also weighed in, saying that Europe's security initiatives 'might not be harmonious with NATO's own expenditures and NATO's needs'.[54]

The pressure worked. The United States was able to peel off individual EU states, especially those located near Russia, thwarting the prospect of EU strategic autonomy. The Ukraine crisis has increased EU dependence on the United States.

Preserving European military dependence

Achieving European strategic autonomy would have been difficult even without the United States sabotaging it. Among the most difficult issues is the question of hierarchy within Europe. Should France or Germany be dominant? Many wars have been fought in Europe to resolve such questions. The United States, through NATO, froze or blocked inter-European rivalries during the Cold War. It did not resolve them.

French President Emmanuel Macron is the most outspoken European advocate of strategic autonomy, with good reason; France's nuclear arsenal would give it ascendancy within the EU. Macron signalled his resolve in March 2022, two weeks after Russia re-invaded Ukraine. He and his nuclear force commanders conducted a nuclear-signalling drill called Exercise Poker. They chose a night when the skies were clear and cloudless. Macron descended twenty storeys beneath Paris to an underground nuclear command-and-control bunker. They waited for a Russian spy satellite to pass over French skies, so it could see what they were doing. Then Rafaele fighter jets took off, with dummy nuclear bombs strapped to their wings, simulating nuclear attacks on an unnamed country. France conducts these nuclear-signalling exercises every few months. It spends billions of dollars each year to maintain its nuclear arsenal of 290 warheads. It operates its nuclear deterrent independently of the United States and produces all the components for it domestically.

Britain will buy US planes with US-controlled source code to drop US-owned nuclear bombs from the air, making it heavily dependent on the US. It has operational nuclear independence because its nuclear-armed Trident missiles are carried on four submarines controlled by its own commanders. The commanders can launch those missiles when the British prime minister gives the order; another country's permission is not needed. The PM writes four identically worded letters to the commanding officers of the four submarines. They contain orders on what to do if UK submarine officers become convinced through certain pre-arranged tests that the UK had already been destroyed. These handwritten 'letters of last resort' are destroyed unopened after the PM leaves office.[55] The United Kingdom would be operationally independent in its final, posthumous act.

However, its nuclear program remains dependent on the United States' nuclear program. Britain obtains its Trident submarine-launched ballistic missiles from a pool of missiles shared with the US Navy. British submarines test-fire the missiles under US supervision near Cape Canaveral in Florida. US laboratories evaluate those missile tests. The US Strategic Weapons Facility at Kings Bay, Georgia, services the missiles.[56] Britain is developing its nuclear warheads in parallel with the United States, and replacing its Vanguard-class submarines as well, but the high cost (US$129 billion) means a trade-off between nuclear and conventional forces.

Europe doesn't need a first-strike capability but rather the deterrence that comes from a second-strike capability. That means an assured retaliation that an enemy cannot prevent even if it overwhelmed Europe with a surprise attack using nuclear-armed missiles. And the only reliable EU delivery vehicle for this assured second-strike retaliation is France's nuclear-armed submarines. But the decision to use those weapons would always remain with the French president, meaning that all European states that relied on a French deterrent would also acknowledge France's primacy in Europe's decision-making councils. It was one thing for them to agree to US supremacy: doing so stalled questions about hierarchy inside Europe. It would be quite another thing to accept France at the top of the European pyramid.

In 2024, on a state visit to Sweden, Macron shared the stage with the king and prime minister of Sweden as he addressed an audience of Swedish military officers and cadets. Sweden had been a neutral country, but it applied to join NATO after the Russian re-invasion of Ukraine. Speaking in English to ensure his words were understood beyond a French and Swedish audience, Macron said that Europe's security had thus far been 'decided by the big guys in the room, not by the Europeans themselves'. That had to change, he said. 'We have to be the one to decide.' A Swedish officer asked him if France, as 'the only EU country with an independent nuclear force', had a special responsibility to defend Scandinavian countries from a threat from the north. Would France be prepared to use its nuclear weapons to defend other European countries and not just France? Macron responded without hesitation, 'Definitely yes. Part of our vital interest has a European dimension, which gives us a special responsibility, given precisely what we have and the deterrence capacity we have.'[57]

For all Macron's eagerness, the most vital questions remain unresolved: would France allow other European states to share nuclear decision making, or would it simply take over the nuclear deterrence role unilaterally? Would France allow its weapons to be extensively redesigned so that they can be launched from non-French submarines and aircraft? And the most important question – would France risk the destruction of Paris as revenge for a Russian strike on Stockholm? Europe has avoided thinking seriously about these questions for decades. It could never be certain that the United States would risk the destruction of New York or Los Angeles as revenge for a Russian attack on a European state – but the fact of NATO meant that the question was not urgent. The Trump administration is determined to prevent such questions arising. Defense Secretary Pete Hegseth told NATO headquarters in February 2025 that Europe must take ownership of conventional security – meaning that the United States would remain in charge of nuclear matters.

Europe remains reliant on the United States in conventional forces, too. Its inability to integrate its militaries independently of the United States has consequences; its armed forces use twenty-nine different types of destroyers while the United States uses only four; seventeen different types of tanks or personnel carriers while the United States uses just one; and twenty different fighter planes compared with just six for the United States. That means repairs, maintenance, spare parts and other vital logistical challenges are very hard to coordinate. During the chaotic 2021 withdrawal from Afghanistan, Europeans needed US help to airlift their own evacuees.[58] France, for all its bravado about an independent nuclear deterrent, is operationally constrained without US combat enablers. On the same day that news of AUKUS broke, Macron announced that a leader of Islamic State in the Greater Sahara had been killed by 'French forces'. In reality, these French forces relied on US transport planes for logistical support, US aerial refuellers for its fighter aircraft, US surveillance drones for reconnaissance and US intelligence to track targets.[59] Macron had no alternative but to accept the loss of his submarine deal with Australia; he needed the United States to continue supporting French operations in western and north-central Africa.

European self-reliance would be costly. A study by two research institutions, Bruegel and the Kiel Institute for the World Economy, concluded that an increase of US$270 billion a year, or about 1.5 per cent of the EU's gross domestic product, would be needed.[60] All EU states would be required to spend at least 3.5 per cent of GDP per year on the military; just five NATO states, one of which is the United States, spend more than 3 per cent now.[61] But money is, in a sense, the easier problem. The central problem is the political will to mobilise Europe's populations and reorient its economies. If Russia attacked a European NATO country, the 100,000 US troops stationed in Europe would be joined quickly by 200,000 additional US troops in armoured units designed for the Eastern European battlefield. If Europeans were to act independently, they would have to mobilise from their populations the fighting capacity of 300,000 troops, with a focus on mechanised and armoured forces.

US forces are not just more numerous; they are also more cohesive. They are organised into corps-sized units with a unified command-and-control structure and are backed by US strategic enablers, including strategic aviation and space assets. Replacing them is much more complicated than forming fifty new brigades by conscripting 300,000 Europeans. The new European troops would have to come from twenty-nine national militaries – with serious risk of inter-country bickering – not from a single country like the United States. One estimate is that stopping a rapid Russian breakthrough in the Baltics would require at least 1,400 tanks, 2,000 infantry fighting vehicles and 700 artillery pieces. This is 'more combat power than currently exists in the French, German, Italian and British land forces combined'.[62] It is easier said than done to replace an alliance that has been designed intentionally to rely on US leadership, strategic enablers, airlift, intelligence and coordination.

Fully aware of Europe's strategic paralysis, the United States has already signalled its intention to deprioritise Europe in favour of China. It will remain in the background with its nuclear deterrent, but its conventional forces will focus on China and the western hemisphere. US Defense Secretary Hegseth distributed his Interim National Defense Strategic Guidance throughout the Pentagon in March 2025. The document was marked 'Secret/No Foreign National' in most passages and signed by him. It described US military priorities in broad detail. China's potential invasion of Taiwan would be the 'exclusive animating scenario that must be prioritized over other potential dangers'. US attention would turn to the Indo-Pacific. It would 'assume risk in other theatres' such as Europe. It would deprioritise militants in Africa and the Middle East; other regional US allies would take on the task of containing Iran. Its concept of how the Pentagon will raise, train and sustain its forces focuses solely on a major power war with China, leaving its European allies to deal with any conventional threat from Russia.[63]

3

Frontline Middle East

ON 22 OCTOBER 2024, James Larsen, Australia's ambassador to the United Nations, delivered a statement on human rights to the UN General Assembly's Third Committee. The General Assembly has six main committees to deal with disarmament, economics, decolonisation and other matters. The Third Committee focuses on human rights questions. Larsen was speaking not only for Australia but on behalf of the geopolitical West: the United Kingdom, the United States, New Zealand, Canada, Japan and several European countries such as France, Germany and the Netherlands.

The context was grave; earlier that morning, the newspapers reported that conditions in northern Gaza, in the Occupied Palestinian Territories, were 'beyond catastrophic', with the UN agency on the ground warning that Israeli authorities had for the fifth consecutive day denied urgent requests to help people trapped under the rubble. A surgeon 'personally performed some surgeries in the street with very little medical equipment'.[1] The World Food Program said that no food aid had entered northern Gaza for two weeks. Israeli human rights groups Gisha, B'Tselem and others said that Israel had adopted a 'starve-or-leave policy'.[2] This siege plan was the work of a retired Israeli major general. It had been presented to government leaders and a parliamentary committee in Israel. Jessica Montell, the head of HaMoked, a Jerusalem-based civil rights advocacy group, denounced the plan as evoking 'battle tactics of the Middle Ages' and 'in blatant contradiction to the foundational principles of the laws of war'.[3] Clearly, these matters were of urgent, direct relevance to anyone concerned about human rights.

Larsen's statement was on an entirely different topic – a two-year-old report by the UN Human Rights Commissioner about China's human rights record in Xinjiang. Australia and the countries on whose behalf he spoke were 'all committed to universal human rights', he said. They had 'ongoing concerns about serious human rights violations in China'. These were 'well-founded concerns', and 'no country is above fair scrutiny of its human rights obligations'.[4]

No country?

Two months before, the Israel–Gaza taskforce in the Middle East branch of Larsen's own Department of Foreign Affairs and Trade (DFAT) had concluded that the humanitarian situation in Gaza was 'catastrophic' and 'among the worst in the world'. The Israeli military operation 'has had a large impact'. Tens of thousands of Palestinians had been killed, 1.7 million people, or 75 per cent of the population, were displaced, and 1.1 million people, or half the population, were facing catastrophic food insecurity.[5] Human rights is always an important matter, but the situation in Xinjiang or Tibet was hardly the most urgent human rights question facing the UN.

For its part, as one commentator said, the Australian Government's public statements on Gaza 'sound like they were assembled by throwing the same handful of word magnets at a fridge' – 'concern', 'deep concern', 'grave concern'.[6] As Foreign Minister, Penny Wong's 'day-to-day job largely consists of repeating the phrase "deeply concerned" whenever Israel commits some new atrocity'.[7] These events show that official pieties about human rights mean little when they do not align with the real goals of US strategy – in this case, military dominance of the Middle East. Israel is protected because its actions further this goal. It is worth dwelling on this subject at some length to uncover what Trump is trying to accomplish. As we will see, Australian policy is designed to demonstrate the nation's relevance to this project.

Control, not access

The control of Middle Eastern oil is the main goal of US strategy for the region. Oil is the most important energy resource in the world and the most frequently traded commodity. Whoever controls it can exercise global influence. Trump's focus on the Middle East isn't new; Lord Curzon, British Foreign Secretary from 1919 to 1924, acknowledged that the Allies 'floated to victory upon a wave of oil' in World War

I.[8] His predecessor, Lord Balfour, held the same view; shortly after he committed the British Government to supporting a Jewish national homeland in Palestine in 1917, he said, 'I do not care under what system we keep the oil, whether it is by a perpetual lease or whatever it may be, but I am quite clear it is all-important for us that this oil should be available'.[9] Walter Hume Long, the First Lord of the Admiralty, informed the Institute of Petroleum Technologists in 1921 that, 'if we secure the supplies of oil now available in the world we can do what we like'.[10]

The same principle operated when the United States replaced the British Empire as the dominant power in the region. During World War II, US Secretary of State Cordell Hull advised the president of the Petroleum Reserves Corporation that 'there should be full realization of the fact that the oil of Saudi Arabia constitutes one of the world's greatest prizes'.[11] When the war ended in August 1945, the US State Department described Saudi Arabia's oil resources as 'a stupendous source of strategic power, and one of the greatest material prizes in world history'.[12] Whenever policy-makers talk about 'democracy', 'human rights', 'the rule of law', 'rogue states', or other similar phrases, these candid acknowledgments of the real rather than declared policy goals should be kept in mind.

Control of oil enables US global dominance. The key to understanding US strategy is to distinguish 'access to oil' from 'control of oil'.

'Access to oil' implies that the United States simply wishes to buy oil like any other country; that it wants oil at a reasonable price. That is emphatically not the reason for its Middle East policy. It has bought oil from Latin American suppliers for more than a century, and US east coast oil refiners (PBF Energy, Phillips 66 and Monroe Energy) have no trouble buying oil from West African suppliers.[13] Despite being a net importer of crude oil, the United States has exported some crude oil for more than 100 years. In recent years, however, US domestic production of shale oil expanded so rapidly that domestic oil producers faced a glut. Oil exports rose quickly after the Obama administration approved a law in 2015 that ensured that 'no official of the Federal Government shall impose or enforce any restriction on the export of crude oil'.[14] Today, the United States is a major contributor to the global oil supply network. Being self-sufficient in oil does not affect its Middle East strategy. The United States wants control, not access.

Veto power

Control of oil means, among other things, controlling the terms on which Japan, France and other industrial rivals can access *their* oil. After World War II, the United States wanted Japan to rebuild its economy but remain subordinated. The postwar US occupation blocked Japan's attempt to rebuild its oil-refining facilities destroyed by Allied bombing. As Yoshi Tsurumi recounts, the oil bureau in General Douglas MacArthur's headquarters was 'heavily staffed with American personnel on temporary leave from Jersey Standard and Mobil' oil corporations. Japan became attractive as a location for oil refineries only after the 'loss of China'; that is, when the Communist Party of China won the Chinese civil war in October 1949. The Allied occupation authorities then permitted Japan to begin reconstructing refineries but ensured they remained dominated by Exxon, Mobil, Shell and Getty Oil.[15]

US policy planners said that it was 'all the more imperative that we retain the ability to control their situation by controlling the overseas sources of supply'. Japan's industrial reconstruction required abundant supplies of energy, and the United States would therefore exercise an indirect influence on Japan's economy even after it ended its military occupation. They planned for controls that were 'adept enough and foolproof enough and cleverly enough exercised really to have power over what Japan imports in the way of oil and such other things as she has got to get from overseas'. This would give the United States 'veto power on what she does need in the military and industrial field'.[16] It could induce its client regimes in the Middle East to raise the price of oil when it wanted to apply pressure on Japan. Today, Japan is the fifth-highest consumer of oil in the world, and relies on imports to meet 97 per cent of its needs.[17] A price increase can harm its dollar reserves, ensuring it stays obedient to US preferences.

Sometimes, the US asks for an oil price increase to assist its diplomacy. In 1986, when the United States wanted to improve its relationship with Iran, it agreed to help increase Iran's oil revenues by increasing the price of oil. Vice President George HW Bush therefore requested Saudi Arabia to cut production.[18] This cut resulted in higher crude oil prices, and Iran's oil revenues increased. 'Security' was said to be the reason for the military spending to protect this set-up; the United States said it was protecting the region from the Soviet Union. But this was largely a pretext; the United States discarded it after the fall of the Berlin Wall in November 1989. The National Security Strategy of President George HW Bush, published in March 1990, admitted candidly, 'In the 1980s, our military engagements – in Lebanon in 1983–84, Libya in 1986, and the Persian Gulf in 1987–88 – were in response to threats to US interests that could not be laid at the Kremlin's door. The necessity to defend our interests will continue.'[19] So much for the Soviet threat; the policy was always about controlling the region and controlling other countries' access to the region's oil. US strategic analysts retained this view in the twenty-first century. The strategist and former National Security Advisor Zbigniew Brzezinski wrote that the United States' military dominance of the Middle East region 'gives it indirect but politically critical leverage on the European and Asian economies that are also dependent on energy exports from the region'.[20]

Control of oil also means control of oil profits. The Arab monarchies have huge investment portfolios in US Treasury securities, banks and corporations. Saudi Arabia, for instance, had a stockpile of around US$140 billion in US Treasury holdings in 2024. Kuwait, another family dictatorship, had a stockpile of more than US$45 billion.[21] Oil-rich US client regimes buy US Treasury bonds, make deposits in US banks and otherwise ensure that some of the dollars they earn from oil sales will flow back to US corporations. They also use their oil profits to buy advanced US weapons systems. This recycling of oil revenues ensures a huge foreign subsidy for high-tech US industry, complementing the massive domestic subsidies it receives when the Pentagon buys up its semiconductors, jet engines, composite materials, computers, robots and advanced manufacturing systems. As Noam Chomsky noted, the high-tech corporate sector is 'protected from market discipline'; unlike ordinary Americans, who are exhorted to be self-reliant, the elite investor class expects 'a powerful nanny state to pour money into their pockets'.[22]

Saudi Arabia and the United Arab Emirates (UAE) are among the largest buyers of advanced US weapons systems. One of the first places Donald Trump visited as president in 2017 was Saudi Arabia, which announced commercial deals and weapons purchases from the United States worth around US$350 billion. Even more purchases are expected to be made when Trump visits Saudi Arabia, Qatar and potentially the UAE in 2025. He said the Saudis had 'agreed to spend close to a trillion dollars in American companies' this time.[23] Qatar is a monarchy with the third-largest proven reserves of natural gas in the world. It hosts the forward headquarters of US Central Command at Al Udeid Air Base, which it built at the cost of over US$1 billion. The Qatar Government will commit more than US$8 billion to expand it from an expeditionary to a permanent base to accommodate more than 15,000 personnel and their aircraft. The country's sovereign wealth fund has committed over US$45 billion in investments in US corporations. Qatar Airways is a major buyer of US commercial aircraft.[24] This system of paying tributes and protection costs will be familiar to students of past imperial arrangements[25] – and to people who watch films about organised crime and its protection rackets.[26]

A qualitative military edge

Despite widespread public discussion about moving away from hydrocarbons and transitioning to renewable energy, oil remains critical to the global economy. Oil consumption after the pandemic has exceeded forecasts, even as electric vehicle sales have grown. Global demand for crude oil grew an average of 1.18 million barrels a day during the three decades from 1991 to 2023. The Covid-19 reduction in demand was a temporary phenomenon. Sales of jet fuel increased despite the widespread adoption of more fuel-efficient aircraft. The business press reports that 'the number of flights and, importantly, the quantity of miles flown have increased so much' that 'jet-fuel consumption is for the first time matching seasonal pre-Covid-19 levels'.[27] The Ghawar oil field in Saudi Arabia is easily the largest conventional oil field in the world. Saudi Aramco, the state-run oil company, owns and operates it. Control of it remains a geopolitical priority.

Saudi Arabia promotes an ultra-conservative, politically inactive form of Islam. Its religious establishment encourages deference to the Saudi royal family, portraying politics as a 'worldly' activity that ordinary, pious Muslims should avoid. The United States – and therefore the United Kingdom and Australia – support Israel because it plays a critical role in ensuring the security of Saudi Arabia and the other pro-US Arab monarchies such as Qatar, Kuwait, Bahrain and the

UAE. Their own security services can protect them from internal democratic challenges, but Israel's muscle can prevent other states assisting those internal forces. US aid preserves Israel's military dominance, ensuring the ongoing control of oil. In 1981, Secretary of State Alexander Haig informed Congress, 'A central aspect of US policy since the October 1973 war has been to ensure that Israel maintains a qualitative military edge'.[28] Every subsequent US administration ensured that Israel's qualitative military edge is preserved.

Israel is the first country in the region to get access to advanced US military technology. When the United States sold F-15 aircraft to Saudi Arabia, it provided Israel with Apache and Blackhawk helicopters and stationed its own military equipment in Israel so that Israel could use it. When it sold Saudi Arabia military equipment that allowed it to convert unguided bombs into all-weather precision-guided bombs, it sold a more advanced version of that equipment to Israel. When it sold F-16 aircraft to the UAE, it provided Israel with advanced radar, anti-radiation missiles and KC-135 refuelling aircraft. US legislation, enacted by the US Congress, requires the United States Government to preserve Israel's regional military supremacy. It therefore always sells more lethal weapons to Israel than to any other Middle East country.[29]

The ANZUS connection

A key pillar of Australian strategy originates in the US policy of controlling Middle Eastern oil. Australia's foreign minister in 1950, Percy Spender, tried to negotiate a Pacific pact with the United States along the lines of NATO. Australia had earned a lot of goodwill by joining the United States in the Korean War, but the United States was not interested in a security treaty with Australia, even though both countries were committed to fight the Communist bloc. Spender had friendly meetings with US officials, but they went nowhere. A breakthrough occurred when he met Field Marshal Sir William Slim, a prominent British official with deep knowledge of Anglo-American global strategy. Slim was visiting Canberra and would later become Australia's governor-general. Slim informed Spender that control of the Middle East was central to Anglo-American strategy in the event of a Third World War. Intercontinental ballistic missiles did not exist then. Air bases in Europe and the United Kingdom would be used to bomb the Soviet Union with nuclear weapons. Air bases in the Middle East would be used to bomb the central parts of Soviet Asia and the industrial areas beyond the Ural Mountains. How would Australia fit into this strategy?

The British thought Australian forces ought to deploy to the Middle East, as they had done in both world wars. Three Australian Army divisions would defend the Suez Canal, the Persian Gulf, the oil fields in the southern part of Iran and British-controlled airfields in Iraq. The USSR and Communist China were land powers and could not threaten Australia, unlike Japan in World War II. Since Japan was occupied by the United States, Australia's best divisions would not be needed at home. But Australian public opinion would be unlikely to accept the idea of Australian forces going to the Middle East, leaving Australia undefended. How, Spender asked his counterparts in the United States, could Australia or, for that matter, New Zealand, 'justify it to their people if seemingly they were leaving Australia and New Zealand divested of troops'?[30] And that is why the United States agreed to the ANZUS Treaty in 1951 – a Pacific pact would provide political cover for the Australian Government to deploy its divisions to the other side of the world.

Australian forces have deployed to the Middle East many times since then – more regularly than in Australia's own region. That is because the real rather than declared goal of Australian defence policy is to demonstrate its relevance to US global strategy. Australian forces participated in one of the longest maritime enforcement operations in history – nearly thirteen years of sanctions against Iraq from 1990 to 2003, and then the invasion of Iraq. More Iraqi civilians may have died because of sanctions than deaths by all weapons of mass destruction throughout history.[31] Iraqi women and girls suffered disproportionately; they were the first to lose jobs, be moved out of higher education, become malnourished and face food insecurity.[32]

The sanctions were so severe that two senior UN officials responsible for administering them resigned in protest. One said the sanctions caused the deaths of between 6,000 and 7,000 children per month.[33] The other called them 'genocidal' and 'a crime against humanity'.[34] A reputable estimate is that they caused between 100,000 and 227,000 excess deaths among young Iraqi children from August 1991 to March 1998.[35] Most commentators on Australian defence policy refer to these maritime enforcement operations but do not mention these figures. They are thus outside the scope of public discussion in Australia. There is every reason to expect that Australia will continue to participate in future US-imposed sanctions programs, as long as domestic constituencies opposed to them remain impotent.

'I'm not sitting in their control room'

The overriding importance of ensuring Israeli military dominance explains the nature of Australia's human rights statements at the United Nations. It is why Defence Minister Richard Marles repeatedly declined to offer a judgment about Israeli operations. An ABC journalist asked him if he agreed with a Labor MP who said that Palestinians were receiving collective punishment. Marles declined to answer, saying he was being asked 'to make a judgement in terms of the rules of war, which can't be made unless you have all the information available to you and you're actually the ones making those decisions, which clearly we are not'.[36] Pressed again over whether Israel was acting within the rules of war, he claimed he couldn't answer the question because 'I don't have all the information available to me that they will have to them, obviously'. Marles added, 'I'm not sitting in their control room'.[37] As we will see, Australia receives timely, accurate and relevant intelligence about the conflict. Television sets can also be purchased in Canberra.

Things were very different for Richard Marles and Penny Wong when they met their US counterparts, Lloyd Austin and Anthony Blinken, in December 2022. The four of them released a strong official statement expressing 'serious concerns about severe human rights violations in Xinjiang, the human rights situation in Tibet', conditions in Hong Kong, crackdowns by the Iranian Government, the Russian invasion of Ukraine, North Korea's human rights violations, and its 'nuclear and ballistic missile programs, which pose a grave threat not only to peace and stability on the Korean Peninsula but also the Indo-Pacific region and the world'.[38]

This is not, contrary to misconceptions, hypocrisy or a double standard. A double standard means that there are two standards, one for minority groups in China, whose human rights the Australian Government cares about, and another for the Palestinians. The reality is that human rights does not motivate foreign policy in either case. The Australian Government talks about Tibet and Xinjiang because it wants to help the United States keep the Chinese Government on the defensive. Otherwise, it would likely ignore them the way it ignores human rights in the Papuan provinces of Indonesia or in the Occupied Palestinian Territories (the West Bank, Gaza and East Jerusalem), or in the United States itself, which has the highest incarceration rate in the world, with 489 prisoners per 100,000 people in 2022.[39] Israel pursues a 'regime of Jewish supremacy from the Jordan River to the Mediterranean Sea' and has been designated an 'apartheid' state by Human Rights Watch, Amnesty International and the Israeli Information Center for Human Rights in the Occupied Territories.[40] Naturally, Australia's foreign policy representatives have no intention of making an international issue out of this.

In 2025, a UN Commission of Inquiry concluded that Israel committed genocidal acts under the Genocide Convention, and under the Rome Statute, which created the International Criminal Court. It found that Israel targeted hospitals and other health facilities in Gaza that provide reproductive services, including an IVF clinic where thousands of embryos were destroyed. It said the Israeli authorities 'destroyed in part the reproductive capacity of the Palestinians in Gaza as a group, including by imposing measures intended to prevent births, one of the categories of genocidal acts in the Rome Statute and the Genocide Convention'.[41] The Commission cited the 'frequency, prevalence and severity of sexual and gender-based crimes' and concluded that 'sexual and gender-based violence is increasingly used as a method of war by Israel to destabilize, dominate, oppress and destroy the Palestinian people'. It 'documented a pattern of sexual violence, including cases of rape and other forms of sexual violence, torture and other inhumane acts that amount to war crimes and crimes against humanity'. It concluded that 'sexualized torture, including rape and violence targeting the genitals, are committed with either explicit orders or an implicit encouragement by the top civilian and military leadership'.[42]

Australia's policy planners are motivated by entirely different concerns. They use a single standard – does something protect or advance US power and Australia's relevance to it? If it does, human rights will be ignored or highlighted as needed. This is not disclosed to the Australian public, of course, perhaps because policy planners fear that ordinary Australians are not willing to support the domination of other people. The policy direction will continue for as long as domestic constituencies opposed to them remain disorganised and ineffective.

Nuclear proliferation

A single standard also applies to nuclear proliferation. North Korea's nuclear and ballistic missile programs are regularly denounced because they are an obstacle to US dominance of the Korean Peninsula, and thus to its ability to position its military bases near the border with China. Australian intelligence agencies have known for decades that Israel possesses nuclear weapons. So does the United States. So does France, which helped Israel obtain those weapons. But Israel performs a major service to the geopolitical West's control of the Middle East, and its nuclear weapons allow it to remain the dominant military power in the region. That is why its nuclear weapons do not attract critical press releases, let alone sanctions.

Australia's intelligence agencies began monitoring Israel's nuclear program from its earliest days in the 1950s, when Shimon Peres, who would become Israel's prime minister, took charge of the program. He obtained plutonium separation technology and a research reactor from France in 1957. He set up the Negev Nuclear Research Center the following year. Israel needed 'heavy water', an industrially produced form of water with a unique atomic structure that is well suited to produce weapons-grade plutonium. It obtained it from Norway in 1959 and began producing plutonium in

1966. That year, Australia's Atomic Energy Commission obtained 'highly sensitive' information from France that the Negev facility contained a large underground chemical reprocessing plant for extracting weapons-grade plutonium from spent reactor fuel.[43]

Australia has known about Israel's nuclear program for nearly sixty years. Twenty years after its discovery of the true purpose of the Negev facility, Australian intelligence advised Labor foreign minister Bill Hayden that 'intelligence assessments are that Israel has a small arsenal of nuclear weapons (possibly about 20). Israel's technological capabilities would enable it confidently to deploy such weapons without recourse to a nuclear test.'[44] That is because Israel had unrestricted access to France's nuclear test data in the 1960s, so much so that France's 1960 nuclear test 'made two nuclear powers, not one – such was the depth of collaboration'.[45]

The US and its allies, including Australia, have gone along with Israel's policy of nuclear ambiguity or *amimut*, a Hebrew word that translates as 'opacity'. They have protected Israel's nuclear program in many ways, including by thwarting public attempts to understand it. In 1996, for example, when President Bill Clinton declassified 1960s- and 1970s-era US spy satellite imagery, a law known as the Kyl–Bingaman Amendment forbade the declassification or publication of satellite images of Israel unless it was at the same level of resolution as could be obtained from commercial sources.[46] The law shielded Israel's nuclear program from civilian analysts for twenty-four years. It also concealed the substantial changes in the Occupied Palestinian Territories caused by Israel's land usage: the destruction of Palestinian structures, the illegal construction of settlements and the growth of military outposts. Finally, in 2020, after commercial satellite providers around the world became advanced enough, the United States permitted images with a resolution of 0.4 metres. Whereas civilian researchers could once see only the broad outlines of a large building, they now see individual cars parked outside.[47]

After the 1967 war, when Israel defeated Egypt and Syria and secured indirect US dominance of the region, the United States decided not to confront Israel about its nuclear weapons. The US National Security Advisor, Henry Kissinger, advised President Richard M Nixon that the United States and Israel had different notions of what it meant to 'introduce' nuclear weapons into the Middle East. The United States considered 'introduction' to mean the 'physical possession and control of nuclear arms'. For Israel, however, 'only testing and making public the fact of possession constitute "introduction"'.[48] Since it hadn't openly tested, publicly declared or used its nuclear weapons, it claimed it had not 'introduced' nuclear weapons into the region. The United States agreed not to make an issue of this stance, nor to pressure Israel to sign the Nuclear Non-Proliferation Treaty – but it had to keep its program restrained and invisible.

Israel has requested every US president from Bill Clinton onwards to sign a letter indicating that US arms control efforts would not affect Israel's nuclear weapons stockpiles. President Clinton signed the first letter as part of an agreement for Israel's participation in the 1998 Wye River negotiations with the Palestinians. The letter stated that no future US arms control initiative would 'detract' from Israel's 'deterrent' capabilities. President George W Bush followed Clinton's lead, signing a similar letter. President Obama signed an updated version of the letter in May 2009. The existence of these letters was a closely guarded secret until President Trump was inaugurated in January 2017. The next month, a delegation of senior Israeli officials visited him, wanting to discuss many topics, one of which was the letter. The *New Yorker* magazine reported in 2018 that neither Trump nor his aides knew anything about the letters and were annoyed at the urgency of the Israeli request. Later, Trump did sign the letter, becoming the fourth consecutive US president to agree in writing not to pressure Israel about its nuclear weapons program.[49] There is no reason to think that Joe Biden did anything different, nor that Trump will diverge from this stance in his second term, unless domestic constituencies mobilise to draw attention to it.

An intelligence leak in October 2024 confirmed that the United States and Australia know important details of Israel's secret nuclear weapons capability.[50] As tensions with Iran rose and Israel said it would strike Iran in response to a missile barrage, two documents marked Top Secret began circulating online. They originated in the US National Geospatial-Intelligence Agency, which is responsible for imagery intelligence from satellites and other overhead assets.[51] The intelligence documents contained releasability markings that indicated they were released to Australia, Canada, New Zealand and the United Kingdom as well. They described Israel's preparations for a strike on Iran and other activities. They identified the exact type of cruise missiles Israel was preparing. They also stated that those missiles would be launched from F-15I aircraft, not the Israel Air Force's F-35 jets. The detail is significant because the F-15I is a modified version of the Boeing F-15E, with greater take-off weight (36,750 kilograms) and longer range (4,450 kilometres) than other F-15 models.[52] It has long been regarded as having a nuclear delivery role.

The documents also discussed Israel's Jericho II medium-range ballistic missiles, which are solid-fuelled and can be launched from silos or from specialised vehicles. The intelligence assessment was that Israel may have dispersed its Jericho II missiles to prevent them being targeted by Iran. They confirmed US knowledge that the Jericho II missiles carry nuclear warheads, stating that 'we have not observed indications that Israel intends to use a nuclear weapon'. The Jericho nuclear missile program dates back to 1963, when Israel signed a contract with French company Dassault to produce a short-range surface-to-surface ballistic missile known as Jericho. The program produced twenty-four to thirty missiles by around 1970. At the time, the US State Department produced a study that concluded that Israel wanted an invulnerable second-strike capability. The study concluded that 'Israel is now building such a force – the hardened silos of the Jericho missiles'.[53] Israel developed the medium-range Jericho II in collaboration with apartheid-era South Africa in the late 1980s.

The leaked intelligence documents show that the US intelligence community monitors Israeli military activity closely and shares its knowledge with Australia. US imagery satellites were able to track a cart that is half the size and width of a sedan across Israel, and to do so for long enough to figure out exactly which type of missile was about to be loaded onto Israel's nuclear delivery aircraft.[54] As such, they show that official pieties about non-proliferation cannot be taken seriously. Israel is assessed as possessing around ninety nuclear warheads for delivery by aircraft, land-based ballistic missiles, and possibly sea-based cruise missiles.[55] Foreign policy is a matter of priorities, and ensuring control of Middle Eastern oil is a higher priority than a nuclear-weapons-free zone in the Middle East. This brings us to the Iranian dimension.

A nuclear-weapons-free zone in the Middle East

In October 2023, Foreign Minister Penny Wong announced new financial and other sanctions on Iranian individuals and entities for their role in Iran's nuclear and missile programs. She said her government was 'working deliberately and strategically to apply pressure on the Iranian regime'. Iran's 'proliferation of ballistic and cruise missiles raises tensions in an already volatile region'. She demanded that Iran 'cease its escalatory actions in its nuclear program and recommit to full compliance with its nuclear-related commitments'.[56] Reducing the proliferation of nuclear weapons is a worthy goal, of course, and there are feasible ways to achieve it. There is considerable support in the Middle East for a nuclear-weapons-free zone that covers the entire region.

Iran first proposed a nuclear-weapons-free zone for the Middle East in 1974, when it was a close US ally and a monarchy. The Islamic Republic replaced the monarchy in 1979, but Iranian leaders continue to indicate their interest in such an arrangement. They would like the entire Middle East to be free of nuclear weapons – themselves, Israel and everyone else. A nuclear-weapons-free zone in the region means intrusive inspections by the International Atomic Energy Agency (IAEA) for all countries. The Arab states are in favour. So are most countries in the world. However, as the IAEA states, 'notwithstanding the continuing broad support' of a nuclear-weapons-free zone in the Middle East, 'there continues to be a lack of agreement among States in the region on the substance and modalities'.[57] The reason is not hard to understand. Israel's nuclear weapons arsenal – the only one in the region – would be confirmed. And the United States will not permit Israel's nuclear arsenal to be subject to international inspection. Australia will therefore continue to avoid talking about Israel's existing nuclear weapons while sanctioning Iran for the possibility that it might be working on a program. Meanwhile, the foreign minister claims that the sanctions 'demonstrate Australia's commitment to the non-proliferation of nuclear weapons, and determination to work with our international partners'.[58] The claims go unchallenged because no domestic constituencies have countered them with facts.

Australia, like the United States, has a special obligation to pursue a nuclear-weapons-free zone in the Middle East. When the UN Security Council did not authorise the invasion of Iraq in 2003, the United States concocted a pretext based on a twelve-year-old Security Council Resolution that ended the 1991 Iraq War. That Resolution, UN Security Council

Resolution 687, noted that Iraq's disarmament actions were to 'represent steps towards the goal of establishing in the Middle East a zone free from weapons of mass destruction and all missiles for their delivery'.[59] Having invaded Iraq on the basis of Resolution 687, the United States and Australia have a special responsibility to pursue a nuclear-weapons-free zone in the Middle East. The absence of effective domestic constituencies means they are under no pressure to do so.

Australian intelligence knows that Iran's nuclear ambitions are defensive rather than aggressive. US State Department cables released by WikiLeaks have shed light on regular intelligence exchanges between Australia and the United States. Australia's peak intelligence analytical agency, the Office of National Assessments (ONA), shared its view of Iran with analysts from the US State Department's Bureau of Intelligence and Research. According to the Director-General of ONA, 'It's a mistake to think of Iran as a "Rogue State"'. Although Iran 'clearly represented the greatest challenge to regional stability, and ONA was focusing most of its attention on Tehran because of it', Australia's analysts appeared to take a calm view of Iran's nuclear program, saying they 'viewed Teheran's nuclear program within the paradigm of "the laws of deterrence"', noting that Iran's ability to produce a weapon may be 'enough to meet its security objectives'.[60]

US intelligence officials have testified to Congress for many years that Iran is focused 'on deterring and, if necessary, defending against external threats, securing Iran's position as a dominant regional power, and ensuring continuity of clerical rule, economic prosperity, and domestic security'. Its 'conventional military strategy is based primarily on deterrence and – if deterrence fails – the ability to retaliate'.[61] Its objectives are 'first and foremost, regime survival ... Iran's military strategy is designed to defend against external threats, particularly from the United States and Israel. Its principles of military strategy include deterrence, asymmetrical retaliation, and attrition warfare'.[62] According to this view, Iran's behaviour in the Middle East 'reflects its defensive military doctrine, which is designed to slow an invasion and force a diplomatic solution to hostilities. Iranian military training and public statements echo this defensive doctrine.'[63]

Iran's ballistic missile program was also focused on defence, not aggression. It never developed or flight-tested a long-range ballistic missile. Nor did it assert a need to build one. It talked up its medium-range missiles but only developed a modest inventory of relatively inaccurate ones, none of which flew after 2012. Instead, it built up its shorter-range missile systems because they were more relevant to its real needs closer to home. According to an expert analysis in 2015, 'Although "death to America" may still be heard during Friday prayers in Tehran, neither the nuclear warhead nor the delivery vehicle for administering such a blow is being built'.[64] It exposed the limits of its arsenal when it launched barrages of missiles against Israel in October 2024. These were mostly intercepted, and analysts gained unprecedented insights into the extent of Iran's capabilities.[65]

US power and influence overrides the wishes of all the other states in the Middle East calling for a nuclear-weapons-free zone. There is a precedent for Israel's ability to disregard the wishes of the entire international community. In 1958, the South African Foreign Minister, Eric Louw, was concerned about growing opposition to apartheid at the United Nations. He sought the United States' protection for his country's apartheid system. He told the US ambassador that

> he wished to be very frank. A specific and strong resolution against South Africa voted for by a majority of nations in the United Nations did not matter so much, as this was to be expected. What mattered perhaps more than all other votes put together was that of the United States, in view of its predominant position of leadership in the Western world.[66]

He gained US support, and although there was a UN arms embargo in subsequent decades, and protests, boycotts and divestment, South Africa could continue with its policies.

Israel too cannot act without US support. In October 2024, Zohar Palti, a former intelligence director of Israel's Mossad intelligence agency, acknowledged that 'Without the U.S. weapons, Israel cannot fight. But it is Israel who takes the risks' and 'knows how to do the job'.[67] The United States supports it as part of an imperial vision: the United States is the imperial power, controlling the region through a sub-imperial power (Israel) and protectorates (oil-rich Arab monarchies). They all work together to militarily constrain Iran in their individual and shared interests.

Israel's military strength remains vital to US strategy. Its proficiency in surveillance technology can help friendlier

Arab regimes stay in power by improving their ability to monitor and control their populations.[68] In times of crisis, the United States gets veto power over who can access Middle Eastern oil and on what terms: energy-rich Arab monarchies can restrict China's access to energy supplies if the United States wishes to coerce it. Their wealth can combine with Israel's industries to create a pro-US power centre. That was the objective behind the Trump-driven Abraham Accords – the treaties signed in 2020 by Israel, the UAE and Bahrain – and Trump will want more of the same.

Until they face a significant domestic political challenge to their foreign policies, the United States and Australia can continue to ensure that Israel remains the sole nuclear-armed state in the Middle East, even as they sanction Iran. Neo-Ottomanisation, with Israel dominating a fragmented and weakened region, has been discussed for a long time.

4

Frontline China

IN MAY 2024, THE Australian warship HMAS *Hobart* was in international waters in the Yellow Sea. An Australian helicopter launched from the ship was suddenly intercepted by a Chinese J-10 fighter, which dropped flares in its path. Australia's Defence Department issued a statement on China's 'unsafe and unprofessional interaction'. The shadow defence minister called China's actions 'provocative and dangerous' and a 'reckless, dangerous and foolish move'.[1] This chapter looks into the incident, and others like it in recent years. It sheds light on Frontline China, which Trump's Defense Secretary, Pete Hegseth, called his 'sole pacing threat'. The United States will defend its homeland, of course, but apart from that, the 'denial of a Chinese fait accompli seizure of Taiwan' is now the Pentagon's 'sole pacing scenario'.[2] That means US commanders are preparing to defend Taiwan from a Chinese takeover, if ordered to do so. The United States plans to increase the number of submarines, bombers, unmanned ships, bunker-penetrating bombs and military logistics in the region. Australia will calculate how best to contribute to this plan, demonstrating its relevance to US objectives.

Preparing the battlespace

The incident occurred in the Yellow Sea, which borders China, North Korea and South Korea. That body of water is named because of its yellowish sand, which originates from China's Yellow River. HMAS *Hobart* was in international waters, meaning that it had as much right to be there as any other ship. It was about 8,500 kilometres from its home base in Sydney but not too far from the port city of Qingdao in China's Shandong province, home to the strategic submarine base at Jianggezhuang. Qingdao is also home to China's Naval Submarine Academy and is a hub of underwater robotics research and development. These are vital assets for the Chinese navy, and it is sensitive to surveillance and intelligence collection activities in their vicinity.

The *Hobart* is one of three guided-missile destroyers in the Royal Australian Navy; the other two are also named after state capitals – HMAS *Brisbane* and HMAS *Sydney*. They are multi-mission warships; they can protect themselves as well as other ships from aircraft and missile attack. They can engage enemy aircraft at ranges greater than 150 kilometres. Their Aegis Combat System incorporates state-of-the-art radar and missiles. Their long-range missiles can attack other ships. They can attack enemy targets on land with a naval gun that carries extended-range munitions. They have cutting-edge sonar systems, decoys, surface-launched torpedoes and other weaponry.[3] They also carry a helicopter for surveillance and anti-submarine warfare – something that China is very sensitive about, given the proximity of its submarine force.

The helicopter that the Chinese fighter jet intercepted was an MH-60R Seahawk. It is fitted with advanced sonar for submarine detection and tracking. It has three torpedoes for anti-submarine warfare operations, and four Hellfire missiles for anti-surface warfare. These helicopters regularly conduct drills and exercises with Australian and US Navy vessels. The Seahawk's weapons, sensors and communications systems extend the range of the *Hobart* destroyer by 450 kilometres. The Seahawk has three primary roles – intelligence, surveillance, reconnaissance; anti-surface warfare (targeting an adversary's surface ships); and anti-submarine warfare.

Australia is highly proficient in submarine detection and tracking. To better understand what that means, we turn to an object that is about a metre long and weighs less than 4 kilograms. It is an expendable, waterborne sensor called a sonobuoy. In essence, it is a microphone designed to operate underwater, mounted on a flotation device (a buoy). It includes a radio transmitter that transmits sounds detected by the hydrophone to an aircraft. The sonobuoys detect acoustic noise from a submarine's turbines, propellers and other machinery. They detect water flowing over the hull of a vessel once it goes above ten knots. They can detect bubbles in the water caused by a submarine's propeller – a phenomenon known as cavitation. They can even detect noises made by the crew inside the submarine.

Each ship or submarine has an acoustic signature akin to a sonic fingerprint, which is used for identification purposes. Analysts compare the signal collected by the sonobuoys with a previously recorded signature. They build a library of acoustic signatures to help them identify a vessel and understand its activities and capability. The library must be updated every six months or so because the signatures change due to age, wear and tear, and modifications to the vessel. Acoustic signals are also affected when the vessel's load changes, as well as changes in water temperature, variations in depth and salinity and the nature of the seabed.[4]

Australia and the United States airdrop sonobuoys by the thousands. The home base of Australia's maritime surveillance aircraft is RAAF Edinburgh in South Australia. No. 11 and No. 292 Squadrons, part of 92 Wing, operate twelve P-8A Poseidon aircraft, which are a modified version of Boeing's 737-800. They prepare the battlespace by acquiring technical intelligence that enables anti-submarine forces to attack enemy submarines at the start of hostilities, if ordered. This is no secret to the Chinese military. But it is largely concealed from the Australian public, who are told that the activities merely constitute 'freedom of navigation' – a benign and reasonable-sounding term. The silence over what 'freedom of navigation' really involves protects the government from democratic accountability, and from debate as to how Australia's intelligence agencies and military should be used. These are questions of politics, not military strategy. There is no reason to withhold this information from the public, at least if national security is to be a goal rather than an alibi. It is not the same thing as intelligence information or operationally sensitive tactics and techniques. The public can decide for itself whether Australia should focus on demonstrating relevance to the United States or some other, more independent defence objective.

Does China have good reason to fear these activities, or is it being unreasonable and aggressive? Does it fear a potential adversary that has threatened it before? The factual record is quite well documented. Scholars and practitioners are aware of it. Sharing it with the public can improve the quality of the national conversation.

Nuclear threats

The United States has threatened China and other countries with nuclear weapons on more than one occasion. China decided to acquire nuclear weapons in response to such threats.[5]

President Truman gave the order to carry out the only nuclear attacks in history – against Hiroshima and Nagasaki in August 1945. The United States planned to drop a third atomic bomb in late August, and potentially several more in September and October 1945.[6] The USSR's entry into the Pacific war resulted in a swift decision by Japan to surrender.[7] Just five years later, during the Korean War (1950–53), Chinese forces were involved in support of North Korea, just as US-led forces supported South Korea. A journalist asked Truman about his military intentions. Truman replied, 'We will take whatever steps are necessary to meet the military situation, just as we always have'. Did that include the atomic bomb? 'That includes every weapon we have', Truman replied. Did this mean there was 'active consideration' of its use? 'There has always been active consideration of its use', Truman replied, adding that it was a 'terrible weapon' that 'should not be used on innocent men, women, and children'.

The White House correspondent for United Press, Merriman Smith, offered Truman a chance to pull back, asking, 'Did we understand you clearly that the use of the bomb is under active consideration?' Truman replied, 'Always has been. It is one of our weapons.' Asked about military versus civilian objectives, Truman said, 'It's a matter that the military people will have to decide. I'm not a military authority that passes on those things.' The correspondent for NBC, Frank Bourgholtzer, asked whether the UN would decide on the use of nuclear weapons, since US-led forces were fighting in Korea under the UN's authority. No, replied Truman, 'The military commander in the field will have charge of the use of the weapons, as he always has'.[8] The United Press wire story went around the world: 'President Truman said today that the United States has under consideration use of the atomic bomb in connection with the war in Korea'.[9] China's military and political leaders took notice.

Truman's successor, President Dwight D Eisenhower, also issued nuclear threats. In May 1953, he authorised an expanded bombing campaign against North Korea. The official Pentagon history notes that his military commanders presented six different scenarios, 'most envisioning the possible use of atomic weapons'. Then, after the US National Security Council reached a consensus on using nuclear weapons tactically and strategically, the United States communicated its intention to China and North Korea. The Pentagon history says that President Eisenhower and Secretary of State John Foster Dulles believed 'the message had the desired effect' of ending the war.

The very next year, there were escalating tensions in the Taiwan Strait. Chinese Nationalist forces in Taiwan faced off against Chinese Communist forces in mainland China. The Nationalists harassed the Communists from islands in the Strait. Chinese coastal batteries began shelling them in 1954. The crisis intensified in January 1955. Secretary of State Dulles said in a nationally televised speech in March that the United States considered atomic weapons 'interchangeable with the conventional weapons'. President Eisenhower and Vice President Nixon made public statements about employing tactical nuclear weapons if war broke out. General Curtis E LeMay, commander of US Strategic Air Command, deployed B-36 bombers to Guam and selected mainland Chinese targets for them. The crisis subsided when China indicated its willingness to negotiate.

A similar crisis occurred in 1958. China moved its forces into Fujian province opposite Taiwan. US officials prepared contingency plans and warned China about its intentions. It prepared a military response, making its B-47 bombers in Guam available for nuclear strikes against China. It also made other plans involving nuclear weapons. The official historian of the US Defense Department said that 'on no other occasion during Eisenhower's second term was [nuclear weapons] use so seriously considered'.[10] The crisis dragged on for another two months until China backed off. Chairman Mao Zedong had already decided after the nuclear threats in 1955 that China needed its own nuclear weapons. It had made a formal decision to do so in January 1955. It successfully detonated its first nuclear device in 1964.

Fear is an important part of the reason for China's extreme sensitivity to foreign military operations near its coastline. In the early decades, China did not develop the southern coastal provinces of Guangdong and Fujian, populated by tens of millions of people, because it expected to have to bomb them with its own air force to stave off an invasion by the United States or the administration in Taiwan. It spent two-thirds of scarce state industrial investment in the 1960s on dispersing and concealing its industries from enemy air attack.[11] Fear drives China to achieve a second-strike capability.

Second strike

A 'second-strike capability' means the ability to retaliate massively to an adversary's surprise, large-scale nuclear first strike. It means that even if an adversary destroys your country, society and government with overwhelming nuclear forces, you can do the same in retaliation. China's policy planners are aware that its land-based ballistic missiles may become vulnerable, given the huge US advantages in precision strike and space-based surveillance capabilities. But submarine-launched ballistic missiles are less vulnerable than other nuclear delivery systems. Their survivability is the most important factor in achieving strategic stability. The key is to possess submarines armed with ballistic nuclear missiles.

China is building a fleet of ballistic nuclear missile submarines, sometimes called the Second Nuclear Force. It wants to reassure the United States that it possesses enough retaliatory capability to end US existence and thereby deter it. In this line of thinking, a US–China relationship based on mutual nuclear vulnerability may 'enhance strategic stability by deterring potential rivals from attempting a nuclear first strike or nuclear coercion in a crisis, and by dissuading any rivals from even attempting to obtain first-strike capabilities against China', according to analysis published by the Carnegie Endowment for International Peace.[12]

Submarine-launched ballistic missiles are deployed on nuclear ballistic submarines (SSBNs). They fly on a ballistic flight path, as do inter-continental ballistic missiles (ICBMs). That means they are launched into flight by a brief burst of rocket power. They then travel in a high, arcing trajectory under their own momentum. They are different from cruise missiles, which are powered continuously and follow a lower, flatter path. China's submarine deterrent consists of six ballistic nuclear missile submarines at the Yalong naval base on Hainan Island. According to the Pentagon's 2023 report on China's military modernisation, China has equipped these submarines to carry either the 7,200-kilometre range JL-2 missile or the 10,000-kilometre range JL-3 ballistic missile.

It has begun replacing the JL-2s with JL-3s as each submarine returns to port for routine maintenance.[13]

If the submarines stay in semi-enclosed, protected waters near China, the JL-2 missile cannot reach the continental United States, only Guam, Hawaii and Alaska. The submarine will have to leave its relatively secure location and sail deep into the Pacific Ocean to launch its missiles if it wishes to hit the continental United States. But it then becomes vulnerable to US and Australian anti-submarine forces. If the longer range JL-3 ballistic missile is used, then a submarine can attack the northwestern parts of the continental United States, but not from the South China Sea. It will have to sail far north, likely to the Bohai Sea, in northern Chinese waters. Even then, it cannot target the US capital, Washington DC, on the far side of the US continent. It must sail past northeast Japan and into the Pacific Ocean if it wants to do that, and then it becomes vulnerable to anti-submarine forces again.[14]

There are two ways to protect these ballistic missile-carrying submarines and make them less vulnerable. One is to make them quieter and stealthier. The other is to operate them from inside a 'bastion' – a heavily defended body of water where an adversary's anti-submarine warfare forces cannot disable them. China employs both methods, but it runs up against hard limits in the first case. The problem appears to be inherent in the design features chosen to build the submarine in the first place; its large missile compartment, skewed propeller and other basic design features make it very difficult to significantly reduce the submarine's noise level. China's submarines are relatively noisy, perhaps noisier than 1970s-era Russian submarines.[15] (Russia's current submarines are much quieter, but even they aren't as quiet as the United States' current generation of Ohio-class SSBNs.[16]) Newer, quieter Chinese submarines are on the way. According to the *Financial Times*, US naval researchers claim that Russia is helping it develop a quieter propulsion system for these boats.[17]

A bastion strategy is likely to be more effective. There have been reports that China's ballistic nuclear missile submarines are almost always accompanied by a protective force when they enter the South China Sea. This force includes warships, aircraft and (it is assumed) attack submarines, all dedicated to track hostile anti-submarine forces. Until China is confident it can evade these forces by entering the deeper waters of the Pacific Ocean, it will opt for a bastion strategy, especially in the South China Sea. This may be one of the reasons for its aggressive behaviour towards countries with competing claims in those waters. China is using substantial maritime forces to defend its undersea bastion, but from other countries' perspective, China is using its power to reject their own territorial claims. Their legitimate concerns could intensify an arms race in East and Southeast Asia.

This brings us to the strategic significance of Taiwan.

Chokepoints

The undersea geography near Taiwan is a chokepoint for China. The United States uses the undersea geography to its advantage, making use of two types of sensors to construct an anti-submarine warfare barrier. The first type is called a Reliable Acoustic Path (RAP) sensor. It consists of thousands of hydrophones mounted at the bottom of the shallow continental shelf. They are connected to each other by fibre-optic cables that come ashore in Philippines and Japanese territory for data processing by US technical intelligence. The sensors can detect even very quiet submarines because there is very little background noise in these locations. At the moment, as we have seen, Chinese submarines are not quiet – far from it. The United States can detect China's submarines as they cross the RAP sensor barrier and trail them covertly with its own very quiet submarines, or use maritime patrol aircraft and ships equipped with antisubmarine warfare helicopters to trail them overtly. US anti-submarine forces can attack them when ordered to do so.

The second type of sensor passively monitors the deep sound channel, a layer in the oceans about a kilometre deep, acoustically isolated from the ocean layers above and below it. Sensors can detect sounds transmitted in the channel from thousands of kilometres away.[18] However, it is very difficult to tell the difference between submarine noise and other background noises in the ocean. That is why sensors monitoring the deep sound channel work in tandem with RAP sensors, which are more precise but have a much smaller range. Together, they constitute five anti-submarine warfare barriers that Chinese submarines must cross: first, when they leave their submarine base to go on patrol; second, when they return; third, a deep sound channel hydrophone barrier; fourth and fifth, anti-submarine warfare screens in each direction from maritime patrol aircraft and ships equipped with antisubmarine warfare helicopters. As two analysts have shown, China could lose two-thirds of its submarine force by the end of its first patrol, and this is a conservative calculation: any Chinese diesel submarine that evaded attack at the first barrier would exhaust its battery reserves during a high-speed escape. It would then have to leave the operating area or come up for air, where it would be vulnerable to further attacks.[19]

China's calculations in light of the above analysis are not hard to comprehend. Its tactical focus is the Bashi Channel, which lies more than 2 kilometres underwater between southern Taiwan and the northern Philippines.[20] It is the only undersea passage for submarines seeking to leave the South China Sea and enter the western Pacific Ocean. It is heavily patrolled by adversarial anti-submarine forces. If China were to incorporate Taiwan, it would not have to worry about the Bashi Channel chokepoint or the RAP barriers near Taiwan. It could simply set up a new submarine base on Taiwan's east coast, near the ports of Keelung, Su'ao, Hualian and Taitung. Doing so would allow it to get around at least three anti-submarine warfare barriers, and perhaps all five. It would be in a better position to deter the United States. Its submarines could go from eastern Taiwan directly into the western Pacific Ocean, no longer needing to traverse 1,240 kilometres of potentially hostile waters.

China lacks deep sound channel hydrophones facing the western Pacific Ocean. This is a serious vulnerability in its defensive perimeter. But, if it were to incorporate Taiwan, it could close that gap by placing and defending hydrophones on the eastern side of Taiwan's coast. It could also install other maritime surveillance assets, giving it a good picture of US naval forces. Chinese cruise missiles could deter US warships from a safe distance. China could then detect and roughly track US surface forces, at ranges at least as far as 1,000 kilometres away. The United States would then have to either move away from harm or escalate to anti-satellite warfare, with the risk of space debris in low Earth orbit, 500 kilometres above the Earth, where thousands of commercial and military satellites now operate. Damage to them would jeopardise the global economy. In effect, China would have achieved its goal of deterring hostile forces off its own coastline. Of course, if China claimed it was 'deterring' Australia by conducting continuous surveillance and intelligence collection patrols just 12 nautical miles off the coast of Fremantle or Sydney, Australians would have no difficulty recognising such behaviour as a pretext for dominance.

Ambiguity in the Law of the Sea

The incidents between Chinese fighter aircraft and Australian warships and helicopters should be understood in this context of submarine versus anti-submarine activities. A strategic analyst noted that Australia's P-8A Poseidon aircraft are 'laden with electronics and sonobuoys, and are customized for anti-submarine warfare'. He adds that 'their known capabilities may simply lead to the assumption by the Chinese military that they are "spying"' even if they are performing routine flights. He suggested that 'Australia's aircraft are being targeted because of their crucial role in submarine detection and the undersea balance of power'. He called for efforts to help the Australian public gain a better understanding of the core interests at stake 'now, rather than in the febrile context of a fatal incident'.[21] It's a good suggestion.

Defence Minister Richard Marles says Australia is acting in accordance with international law when conducting naval and aviation activities in China's exclusive economic zone (EEZ). These activities in the South China Sea and the other semi-enclosed waters off the coast of China are usually described in vague terms such as 'freedom of navigation'. What does that term really mean? What activities does it cover?

The United Nations Convention on the Law of the Sea (UNCLOS) has been called a 'Constitution for the Oceans'.[22] It came into force in 1994 after many years of painstaking negotiations. It gives Australia, China and other states with coastlines the exclusive right to explore, exploit, conserve and manage all natural resources in the waters overlying the seabed, as well as the seabed and its subsoil, out to 200 nautical miles from their coasts. These are called exclusive economic zones. The United States participated in negotiations that led to the Convention, but President Ronald Reagan did not sign it. In 1994, the United States signed the Convention under President Clinton but has never ratified it. China has signed and ratified it, and has benefited from the US absence. As it is a member, it can appoint a judge to the International Tribunal for the Law of the Sea and take a leading role in the other institutions created by the Convention, such as the International Seabed Authority.

A country may conduct military exercises and practise its intelligence collection efforts inside its own territorial waters, and even in its own EEZ. But when it enters another country's EEZ, does international law allow it to fly maritime surveillance aircraft, drop sonobuoys and engage in activities that allow the preparation of battlespace to gain an advantage in a looming conflict? UNCLOS is silent on this important question – can a country do all this in another country's EEZ? China says no: it says ordinary navigation and transit are fine, but it objects to what it calls 'military freedom of navigation', another term for non-economic military hydrographic and oceanographic surveys. China's concern is about US Navy vessels and aircraft, not civilian ones. It benefits from ordinary navigation and transit, which it relies on for its own trade routes. Its ambassador to the Philippines stated succinctly, 'no freedom of navigation for warships and airplanes'.[23] Admiral Sun Jianguo of China's Central Military Commission said that this kind of activity 'brings with it a military threat'.[24]

China is not isolated in its view, according to security scholar Oriana Skylar Mastro. She observes that:

> Argentina, Brazil, India, Indonesia, Iran, Malaysia, the Maldives, Oman and Vietnam agree with China that warships have no automatic right of innocent passage in their territorial seas. Twenty other developing countries (including Brazil, India, Malaysia and Vietnam) insist that military activities such as close-in surveillance and reconnaissance by a country in another country's EEZ

> infringe on coastal states' security interests and therefore are not protected under freedom of navigation.[25]

The United States, Australia and the United Kingdom and some other states disagree. However, 'freedom of navigation' doesn't explain the real reason, which is that the United States wants to project power around the globe. Its focus is wider than China; it wants to dominate the Persian Gulf against adversaries like Iran, and the waters in every other EEZ around the world, against every potential adversary. If an international consensus were to crystallise against its position, the United States would have to conduct its battlespace preparations ('freedom of navigation') outside of the 200-mile EEZ of an adversary, not the 12 miles of territorial sea. That would limit its global dominance.

Priorities

Cables released by WikiLeaks explain how deeply opposed Australia is to the rights of coastal states – even when Australia is the coastal state. In October 2006, the Howard government imposed a compulsory pilotage regime to reduce the risk of oil and chemical spills in the fragile marine environment of the Great Barrier Reef. The regime required vessels to use a pilot to navigate the narrow channel of the Torres Strait, an area of biogeographical importance where two ocean systems meet – the Coral Sea (Pacific Ocean) and the Arafura Sea (Indian Ocean). It is a vulnerable ecosystem, with extensive seagrass beds, dugong and turtle populations, coral reefs, and mangrove islands. The area falls inside Australia's and Papua New Guinea's exclusive economic zones. It also includes some of their internal waters and territorial sea. It is home to indigenous Australian and Papua New Guinean citizens who depend on the marine environment for subsistence fishing and gathering. They are so reliant on the environment that they have the highest seafood consumption in the world.[26]

However, Singaporean diplomat Tommy Koh told the US ambassador in Singapore that his government was 'deeply concerned' that Australia's actions would encourage 'other coastal states to encroach on the right of free passage as enshrined in the UN Convention on the Law of the Sea'. Singapore's foreign minister also complained to the Australian Government about the 'negative impact on larger strategic interests'.[27]

Australia had legitimate concerns about the risk of an environmental catastrophe. The head of DFAT's International Legal Division told the American Embassy's economic counsellor that more than 130 oil tankers had passed through the Torres Strait in 2007. Australia was worried they 'could be involved in an accident causing environmental damage to the area'. Prime Minister Rudd, he said, had told Singaporean Prime Minister Lee Hsien Loong that it was 'politically impossible to change the mandatory nature of the regime. If there were to be an oil spill after the Rudd Labor Government "weakened" the environmental protections imposed by the Howard Government, ... the political cost would be immense.' He wanted to find a solution and 'everything is on the table ... except the mandatory nature of the regime'.

The United States replied by saying that the compulsory pilotage scheme was 'the exact point which we find unacceptable'.[28] The United States supported Singapore's positions over Australia's, complaining to Australia and urging other countries to protest as well. The Rudd government decided to leave the compulsory pilotage regime in force while agreeing to not enforce penalties against ships that disobeyed it, provided they did not subsequently call at an Australian port. Australia thus weakened its compulsory pilotage regime for large vessels, such as oil tankers, chemical tankers and liquefied natural gas carriers, potentially endangering the northern side of the Great Barrier Reef.

The Australian Government did not fight for its position, although the Marine Environment Protection Committee had recognised the merits of the case.[29] The Australian Maritime Safety Authority announced the change by publishing a one-paragraph 'Marine Notice' at the bottom of a longer notice on 'Bridge Resource Management'.[30] Labor's transport minister at the time made no public statement about the change.[31] He would become prime minister of Australia in 2022 and 2025.

China's nuclear buildup

As we have seen, China is trying to deploy the JL-2 and JL-3 missiles, with ranges of 7,200 kilometres and 10,000 kilometres respectively, on its newer, stealthier submarines. It is also adding multiple warheads to its arsenal of intercontinental ballistic missiles. Expert analysis by the Federation of American Scientists' Nuclear Information Project estimates that China has a stockpile of approximately 410 nuclear warheads for delivery by land-based ballistic missiles, sea-based ballistic missiles and bombers. It is expected to have about 1,000 operational nuclear warheads by 2030, fielded on systems capable of reaching the continental United States. China's aim is to possess a massive nuclear retaliatory capability known as an 'assured destruction capability' in the language of nuclear strategy. Put simply, it wants to ensure it cannot be intimidated by other countries' nuclear threats. Its nuclear program thus falls within the paradigm of the principles of deterrence.

An important task for China, and one the international community will increasingly insist on, is to provide clarity about the strategic objectives behind its nuclear weapons and submarine programs. Why is it building these up? A declaration that it seeks a limited, second-strike capability will allow outsiders to assess whether its actions are consistent with those objectives. Otherwise, they are likely to entertain their own fears that China has other, more sinister goals such as expansion and conquest. The United States would also have to clarify its policy towards China's deterrent. If they declare formally that they seek strategic stability, then a first step may be to stop conducting strategic anti-submarine tactics against China's ballistic nuclear missile submarines in China's own EEZ. Australian and regional countries can seek clarity and reassurance through diplomatic efforts.

An under-appreciated reason for China's nuclear weapons program is that developments in target detection and weapons delivery systems are making nuclear arsenals around the world more vulnerable. Sometimes called the sensing and precision revolutions, these developments allow a tiny number of technologically advanced countries to find and destroy opposing nuclear forces – a strategy known as 'counterforce'.[32] Remotely piloted aircraft, small satellites and machine-learning algorithms are making it possible to deploy large networks of space-based radars to find other countries' mobile missiles, fixed silos, strategic airbases, submarine ports, command-and-control systems and leadership bunkers. Synthetic aperture radars have tilted the hide-and-seek balance in favour of the seekers. They bathe the ground with radio waves at wavelengths much longer than the visible spectrum, allowing detection of targets at night and through clouds and camouflage netting.

The US nuclear war-fighting strategy has been explicitly focused on counterforce for the past decade. It doesn't prioritise nuclear targeting of an adversary's cities, economic and industrial infrastructure, energy and communication systems, ports or transportation nodes, an approach known as 'countervalue'. In 2013, the Pentagon officially stated that the United States would 'maintain significant counterforce capabilities against potential adversaries'.[33] Among other things, that means preemptively striking an adversary's command-and-control infrastructure and its nuclear forces before they can be launched. China's military strategists understand all this, which is why China is expanding its missile silo fields. Its nuclear buildup can thus be understood as a defensive approach that reduces the pressure to escalate out of fear that it may be suddenly disarmed by a 'bolt from the blue' counterforce attack.

North Korea, which lacks China's wealth and therefore cannot take similar measures, has good reason to be worried. In his first term, President Trump took a less aggressive approach to North Korea than previous US presidents. He did not try to block moves by South and North Korea to lower tensions. The two sides issued the Panmunjom Declaration, which 'affirmed the principle of determining the destiny of the Korean nation on their own accord' and presented a program on how to move forward.[34] As well as not undermining the Panmunjom Declaration, he called off military exercises that had been scheduled, calling them 'very provocative'. He did not ask for concessions beforehand, saying that he wanted 'at some point' to withdraw the US troops currently in South Korea.[35] It is unclear how he or the policy planning team around him will act in his second term. For this reason, we turn to an examination of what a US nuclear strike would involve.

Nuclear brinkmanship

During the chaotic events of January 2021 at the US Capitol, Speaker of the House Nancy Pelosi wrote to her Democratic colleagues about an extraordinary conversation she'd had with the Chairman of the Joint Chiefs of Staff, General Mark Milley. She said she spoke to him 'to discuss available precautions for preventing an unstable president from initiating military hostilities or accessing the launch codes and ordering a nuclear strike'. General Milley in turn said through a spokesman only that he 'answered her questions regarding the process of nuclear command authority'.[36] Since no further details were disclosed about what this meant, I provide them below.

There is no law that limits the US president's authority to launch a nuclear strike. He has sole authority. No additional officials are needed to co-sign an order. The president, and only the president, can order a nuclear launch, and no one can legally stop him or her.[37] Vipin Narang, later a senior US Defense official, explained that there was no substance to reports that Pelosi had received assurances of safeguards if President Trump wanted to launch a nuclear weapon. Any safeguard would itself be illegal. Presidents are under no legal obligation to consult with White House advisers, the US military chiefs, the defense secretary and others. Even the vice president is not in the nuclear launch chain of command. All the pre-planned nuclear target packages have already been vetted by United States Government lawyers for legality – more correctly, for conformity with US domestic law. Anyone who tried to insert themselves into the chain of command by revoking a presidential order, or refusing to obey it, would risk prosecution for mutiny.

How does the US president order a nuclear strike? A military aide who carries a leather-bound aluminium briefcase is always near the president. Inside the briefcase, which weighs about 20 kilograms, are laminated sheets with dozens of nuclear war plans, targeting options and nuclear strike packages. The briefcase also contains a secure satellite phone. Everything about the briefcase is deliberately low-tech, to minimise technical difficulties. The president would take out a sealed plastic card about the size of a thickened credit card, known as the 'biscuit'. This is an authenticator, which the president carries on his person. It contains alphanumeric authentication codes that will verify his identity. The vice president has an identical biscuit if the president is incapacitated for some reason. Both individuals receive a briefing about nuclear procedures from the US military prior to taking the oath of office.

The president would summon his military aide, who is always nearby. The aide opens the briefcase, also called the 'nuclear football', and connects the president directly to the duty officer at the National Military Command Center, a hardened bunker located underneath the Pentagon. The president would authenticate himself to the duty officer using an alphanumeric code on the 'biscuit'. He would then order one or more of the many nuclear strike packages available to him. The duty officer would check that the president did in fact respond with the correct alphanumeric code, and that the strike package is valid. If so, the order is authentic, and the duty officer is required to transmit that lawful order from the commander-in-chief of the United States directly to the strategic bomber force or a land-based nuclear missile crew or the commander of a submarine armed with ballistic missiles.

Australia could play a vital role in the transmission of those orders. The United States may send them via the very low frequency communications station known as the Harold E Holt Naval Communications Station at North West Cape, near Exmouth in Western Australia. After the order from the president, the National Military Command Center sends a code to unlock a safe inside the submarine containing the launch keys. The submarine crew will then execute the order and conduct the nuclear attack. The communications facility in Western Australia has been in operation since 1967. Its presence rests on a 2008 treaty that gives the United States access to and use of North West Cape for the next twenty-five years. The US system of sole authority allows the president to act quickly and unilaterally. It is a system that has its origins in the Cold War. There have been calls for reform but, as it stands, the US president retains sole authority.[38]

It has long been part of US strategic thinking to portray itself as a little irrational when it comes to nuclear weapons. In 1995, the United States Strategic Command produced a document known as 'Essentials of post–Cold War deterrence'. It argued that it would be better for nuclear deterrence if US leaders did not

> portray ourselves as too fully rational and cool-headed. The fact that some elements may appear to be potentially out of control can be beneficial to creating and reinforcing fears and doubts within the minds of an adversary's decision makers. This essential sense of fear is the working force of deterrence. That the US may become irrational and vindictive if its vital interests are attacked should be a part of the national persona we project to all adversaries.[39]

As such, President Trump is not radically different to previous US presidents.

The same study said that 'nuclear weapons always cast a shadow over any crisis or conflict in which the US is engaged'.

A nuclear-armed country threatened by the United States would not know if the threat was real or a bluff. If it assumed the worst, which isn't unlikely, it could take steps to protect itself, and that could create a potentially lethal competitive spiral. If a war were to break out, the United States would be faced with a problem of a different kind; as an imperial power with a global presence, it will not want to give the impression to adversaries and allies in other theatres that it would back off if another nuclear-armed country tried to deter it. There would therefore be intense pressure to escalate. Wars contain elements of the irrational: pride, fear, confidence, humiliation, and other emotions that elude attempts at calculation. Wherever they start, they finish only when one side decides to give up. The irrational elements thus make direct large-scale confrontation between two nuclear powers very dangerous.

An unsinkable aircraft carrier and submarine tender

Today, within the Indo-Pacific region, there are 375,000 US personnel at sixty-six military sites. US strategy has long been to establish and defend military bases as close to enemy territory as possible. That is why the US Navy's largest forward home-porting location is in Yokosuka, Japan, about 70 kilometres south of Tokyo. It hosts the aircraft carrier USS *Ronald Reagan*, nine Arleigh Burke–class guided-missile destroyers, and three Ticonderoga-class guided-missile cruisers. About 650 kilometres south of the Japanese main islands is the prefecture of Okinawa, which hosts the US Marine Corps' largest combat unit stationed overseas, the III Marine

Expeditionary Force. More than 50,000 active-duty US military personnel are permanently assigned to Japan.

Just as the United States can use NATO to project force against the Eurasian land mass from the west, its military alliances with Japan and South Korea allow it to project force against that land mass from the east. Australia has joined South Korea and Japan as a US sentinel state, attempting to hold Chinese naval assets at risk in their own semi-enclosed seas. Taiwan's location also enables this goal. China's actions are in response to these hostile capabilities.

An important part of the strategic and historical context is US General Douglas MacArthur's farewell speech to Congress. MacArthur oversaw the surrender ceremony in Tokyo Bay, Japan, at the end of World War II. He commanded the Allied occupation of Japan from 1945 to 1951 and made his last official public appearance in a farewell speech to the US Congress in April 1951. That speech is usually remembered today for its peroration ('Old soldiers never die; they just fade away'). However, he also discussed the strategic potential of Taiwan (then known as Formosa) as part of a US strategy to position its bases and forces as close to the edge of China as possible. He called Taiwan 'an unsinkable aircraft carrier and submarine tender'.[40] Thanks to our Pacific victory, he said:

> Our strategic frontier … shifted to embrace the entire Pacific Ocean, which became a vast moat to protect us as long as we hold it … Indeed, it acts as a protective shield for all of the Americas and all free lands of the

> Pacific Ocean area. We control it to the shores of Asia by a chain of islands extending in an arc from the Aleutians to the Marianas held by us and our free allies. From this island chain we can dominate with sea and air power every Asiatic port from Vladivostok to Singapore and prevent any hostile movement into the Pacific.[41]

MacArthur's words are valuable because they express well an assumption that is usually unstated: 'Dominating with sea and air power every Asiatic port from Vladivostok to Singapore' is benign and defensive, if the United States does the dominating. 'Under such conditions,' he said,

> the Pacific no longer represents menacing avenues of encroach for a prospective invader – it assumes instead the friendly aspect of a peaceful lake. Our line of defence is a natural one. It envisions no attack against anyone nor does it provide the bastions essential for offensive operations, but properly maintained would be an invincible defence against aggression.

Taiwan (Formosa) was critical to US dominance of the region: 'under no circumstances must Formosa fall under Communist control'.

What would happen if China controlled an island just 100 miles from its coast? According to MacArthur, the United States, 5,000 miles away, would be threatened: 'Such an eventuality would at once threaten the freedom of the Philippines and the loss of Japan, and might well force our

Western frontier back to the coasts of California, Oregon and Washington'. To accept this pronouncement as an objective analysis of reality, one would have to accept that the United States feels secure only if it can 'dominate with sea and air power every Asiatic port from Vladivostok to Singapore'. That is because it cannot be reassured by China's intentions but must plan for its capabilities. However, China need not plan to counter US 'domination' because it should be reassured by the United States' intentions, which are said to be benign. As MacArthur said, under US control, the Pacific Ocean has 'the friendly aspect of a peaceful lake', since the United States 'envisions no attack against anyone'.

This view is still very much part of US strategy. Seventy years later, the United States continues to describe Taiwan as 'a critical node within the first island chain ... from the Japanese archipelago down to the Philippines and into the South China Sea ... anchoring a network of US allies and partners'.[42] The word used nowadays is not 'dominate', however. It is 'deter'. 'Deterrence' has a non-ideological meaning, but it is often used as a euphemism for dominance. If China claimed it was 'deterring' Australia by conducting non-stop surveillance and intelligence collection patrols just off the coast of Fremantle or Sydney, others would recognise 'deterrence' as a euphemism for 'dominance'. The same logic applies when Australia's politicians claim they are 'deterring' China in waters very close to its coastline, oblivious to the consequences of the positions they advocate.[43]

5

Demonstrating relevance: The strategic logic of AUKUS

AUSTRALIA'S DEFENCE MINISTER RICHARD Marles praised 'the rock-solid commitment of our US and UK partners to the *nation-building* AUKUS program'. Minister for Defence Industry Pat Conroy called it a '*nation-building* endeavour'.[1] Shadow Defence Minister Andrew Hastie said that AUKUS is 'a *nation-building* task that will span generations. It will span governments. It will span parliaments.'[2] This chorus of establishment voices – basically interchangeable with anyone else who might occupy those portfolios – all make the same claim of AUKUS.

The political leadership weren't the only ones to talk about 'nation-building'. The Chief of Navy, Vice Admiral Mark Hammond, urged Australians to ignore 'hand-wringing' doubters of the AUKUS pact. He 'implored Australians to see it as a *nation-building* endeavour on a par with the original creation of the Snowy Mountains Hydro-electric scheme'. He said that the 'national psyche should be proud of its track record of tackling complex challenges and setting global standards'.[3] The Director-General of the Australian Submarine Agency, Vice Admiral Jonathan Mead, said that the '*nation-building* program will be the most transformative industrial and technical endeavour in our history'.[4]

What do we make of the Defence sector's vocal but hitherto unsuspected commitment to nation-building? And its references to the Snowy Mountains Scheme?

Nation-building

We turn to the period after the end of World War II. Australia's remoteness from the major battlefields ensured that its industrial production and agricultural capacity remained intact. It could find large export markets to supply Europe, whose economies were being reconstructed after the war. There was a sense of optimism about the future.

The Snowy Mountains Scheme was one of the largest and most complex engineering projects in the world. It diverted the water from the rivers through tunnels in the mountains, stored it in dams, then used it to create electricity. It employed more than 100,000 people, at a time when the population of Australia numbered only around ten million. Those workers built power stations, dams, aqueducts, tunnels, and 1,600 kilometres of roads and train tracks. The project delivered consistent power supply to help Australia industrialise. The postwar Labor government implemented plans for full employment, created public housing and announced it would take in 70,000 immigrants each year. One of the most recognisable features of this ambition was the first wholly Australian-manufactured car, the Holden, introduced in November 1948. The policy promoted manufacturing, helping to diversify the economy away from sheep, wheat and minerals. It resulted in an expansive period for the Australian economy and Australian culture.

But the purchase of nuclear-powered submarines bears little resemblance to genuine nation-building along the lines of Australia's postwar reconstruction, particularly if we consider the available alternatives and the wider context.

An alternative: Air-Independent Propulsion submarines

At the outset, it must be emphasised that submarines are an essential defence capability for a maritime nation like Australia. They raise the stakes for any adversary contemplating hostile action against us. Submarines are expensive, but countermeasures against them are much more expensive. They allow the government to act at a time of its choosing and under any realistic threat scenario. However, Australia's defence interests would be better served by conventionally powered submarines, not nuclear-powered ones. Air-Independent Propulsion (AIP) submarines are a proven technology. They use oxygen or hydrogen fuel cells to convert chemical energy into electric power at high efficiencies, allowing them to stay submerged for longer periods without the need for external sources of oxygen. They can lurk in an area, submerged and virtually undetectable, for weeks.

In our region, Japan, South Korea and Singapore use AIP boats. Norway, Sweden, Germany, Spain, Portugal and Italy also use them, as does Israel, a nuclear-armed state. South Korea's Dosan Ahn Chang-Ho class and Son Won-Il class submarines use AIP technology. The Dosans can remain submerged for about twenty days continuously and can fire submarine-launched ballistic missiles, torpedoes and naval mines. The Son Wons can remain submerged for about fifty days continuously and can fire torpedoes and anti-ship missiles.[5] The German Type 212A AIP submarine is built of non-magnetic steel that is impervious to magnetically initiated mines and torpedoes and is also harder to detect. It is propelled in the mission area by hydrogen fuel cells, has a crew of twenty-seven, including eight officers, and is much more habitable than earlier boats; instead of hot bunking, there are now dining and working spaces separated from the sleeping quarters.[6] Germany has exported AIP submarine technology to Israel, South Korea and Singapore, and has partnered with Norway in a combined production venture.[7]

Spain's state-owned ship-building company, Navantia, has also innovated with AIP boats based on a classic single-hull 'teardrop' hull form, optimised for stealth. They can remain submerged for up to three weeks using bioethanol reforming technology. They can launch electrically powered heavyweight wire-guided torpedoes, anti-ship missiles, and Tomahawk tactical land-attack missiles.[8] Italy's Todaro-class submarines also have AIP and can remain submerged for about a month without surfacing.[9]

It simply isn't the case that nuclear-powered submarines are the only option available to Australia – unless the real goal of Australia's defence policy is to demonstrate our nation's relevance to the United States. It is analogous to buying a car – how and where you plan to use it informs your choice. Your other spending priorities matter, too. The 'best car' isn't necessarily the most expensive one.

AIP boats are considerably cheaper than nuclear-powered boats, meaning many more could be purchased, with more local maintenance jobs throughout the life of the boats. As former submariner and senator Rex Patrick has argued, Australia could have twenty modern, off-the-shelf submarines built in Australia and enhanced by Australian industry, for $30 billion – much less than nuclear-powered boats: 'Buying them would free up funds so that Australia can acquire more fighter jets, a $40 billion industry resilience package, a national shipping fleet, long-range rockets and other artillery systems, utility helicopters, shoulder-fired anti-aircraft missiles, and more'.[10]

Buying AIP submarines also means buying an item that has been proven at sea. If the goal were really 'nation-building', even within narrow military constraints, then AIP submarines and the diverse array of other equipment would be up to the task.

Nuclear proliferation

Nuclear-powered submarines create another problem. When the nuclear-armed states signed the Nuclear Non-Proliferation Treaty, they insisted on exempting fissile materials used in nuclear-powered ships and submarines from inspection by the International Atomic Energy Agency (IAEA). They wanted to preserve the secrets of their naval reactor designs. US naval nuclear reactors – the kind that will be used by the nuclear-powered AUKUS boats – use weapons-grade uranium that can be used to build a nuclear bomb. All this is often presented as something too technically difficult for ordinary people to understand. It isn't; the average person can understand the basic ideas. Let us demystify them.

Weapons-grade uranium refers to uranium enriched to 93.5 per cent. Enrichment begins with digging up uranium ore from the ground. Almost all this uranium – 99.3 per cent of it – is Uranium-238, which decays very slowly and is barely radioactive. But 0.7 per cent of it is Uranium-235, which can be split under certain conditions, yielding a massive amount of energy. One kilogram of uranium ore has 993 grams of U-238 and 7 grams of U-235.

Enrichment means removing the U-238, usually by heating it at the enrichment plant to turn it into a gas known as uranium hexafluoride, commonly called 'hex'. The gas produced is forced through a centrifuge, which is a machine with a cylinder that spins rapidly, faster than 50,000 times a minute. The heavier U-238 gets concentrated at the outer part of the cylinder and the U-235 at the centre. The slightly enriched gas from one cylinder is fed into the next and subsequent cylinders in a cascade for further enrichment. Meanwhile, the slightly depleted gas is fed back to the beginning of the cascade to be centrifuged again. A large amount of depleted hex is produced as a byproduct of the enrichment process. It can be re-enriched or converted to depleted uranium (DU), a very dense metal that can be used to make penetrating weapons such as bullets and tank ammunition. The U-235 that is left is said to be 'fissile', meaning that it can be used to build a nuclear bomb. The US Navy's reactors use about 100 nuclear bombs' worth of highly enriched uranium every year, more than all the world's other reactors' production combined.[11]

A civilian nuclear reactor – the kind that generates electricity for peaceful purposes – typically uses 3 to 5 per cent enriched uranium as fuel. The enriched 'hex' from the centrifuge is converted back to a solid uranium oxide, producing a ceramic powder which is used to form solid ceramic fuel pellets, each with a diameter of around 1 centimetre. Multiple pellets are encased within individual metal fuel rods. Multiple fuel rods are arranged into complete fuel assemblies. This ceramic fuel is not directly transferable to weapons construction.

By contrast, naval nuclear reactors must be very compact because space is at a premium in submarines and ships. Naval nuclear reactors must also have a long core life – thirty to forty years for submarines and fifty years for aircraft carriers. The fuel composition in these reactors is not ceramic but metallic, with a uranium-zirconium or uranium-aluminium alloy design. This design is directly transferable to build a nuclear weapon. No further enrichment is needed to build a nuclear weapon. AUKUS means that Australia will effectively possess a nuclear weapons capability. Australia will become the first non-nuclear-armed state to acquire nuclear-powered submarines and these submarines require the same high-grade uranium as the rest of the US fleet. There are consequences for this choice.

The AUKUS Treaty says that the United States or the United Kingdom will transfer weapons-grade, highly enriched uranium – described as 'Special Nuclear Material' – contained in complete, welded Power Units to Australia.[12] Australia currently has a Comprehensive Safeguards Agreement with the IAEA to manage its civilian nuclear activities. It allows Australia to negotiate with the IAEA for an arrangement whereby the IAEA oversees the use of nuclear material for naval nuclear propulsion.[13] But the AUKUS Treaty also states that Australia has agreed not to disclose to the IAEA any information about the design, manufacture, operation, maintenance or repair of the naval nuclear reactors.[14] That means Australia wants the IAEA to conduct no more than periodic inspections of the welded Power Units, and only to ensure they have not been tampered with.

The Australian Government understands that all this creates a precedent that will allow Iran, Brazil, South Korea and other countries to develop or acquire nuclear-powered vessels too, enjoying similar exemptions from inspection by the IAEA. Other members of the IAEA, such as China and Russia, can be expected to argue that Australia is a wealthy, sophisticated country with enough technical capability to open the nuclear reactor and divert the highly enriched uranium to make a nuclear weapon, if it chooses. China has raised AUKUS as an issue before the General Conference and Board of Governors of the IAEA, and also at sessions of the Preparatory Committee for the 2026 Non-Proliferation Review Conference. It stated that AUKUS 'poses serious nuclear proliferation risks' and demanded an 'intergovernmental process' involving all IAEA members with any new arrangement 'jointly discussed and decided by the international community'.[15] As national security expert Philip Dorling says, China and Russia 'will likely vote against any arrangement regardless of its terms ... A fractious dispute could drag on for years.'[16]

Australia has therefore committed an extra A$75 million for nuclear diplomacy. That means Australia will engage with the IAEA Secretariat and the thirty-five countries on the IAEA Board, and will lobby all 176 member countries – a diplomatic effort of the level required to run for a seat on the UN Security Council. Australia will fund projects, seminars and workshops to convince the international community that it isn't weakening the global non-proliferation regime. This is all very far from a nation-building project. It is an empire-strengthening project. The public may well support it, of course, but the government hasn't placed its real goals and policies before the public in a meaningful way.

Funding the US Navy's nuclear ballistic missile submarine program

The United States has, since the 1960s, possessed three types of strategic nuclear delivery vehicles: land-based intercontinental ballistic missiles (ICBMs), long-range heavy bombers and nuclear-powered ballistic missile submarines. They are collectively referred to as the 'triad', with the ballistic missile submarines representing the most survivable leg of the triad. As we have seen, they give the United States an assured second-strike capability, which is a deterrent against another country's first strike. At any given moment, some of these ballistic missile submarines are on patrol somewhere in the oceans. A ballistic missile is powered at the start, for durations of a few seconds to a few minutes. It then flies unpowered towards the target. The United States also operates nuclear-powered multi-mission submarines that are conventionally armed. That is what the AUKUS deal refers to. These boats perform a variety of peacetime and wartime missions.

The US Navy currently has fourteen Ohio-class nuclear-powered ballistic missile submarines, each one carrying submarine-launched ballistic missiles (SLBMs) armed with multiple nuclear warheads, ready to be launched from vertical launch tubes in the middle section of the boat. Although each submarine is designed to carry twenty-four SLBMs, four launch tubes have been deactivated as part of an arms control agreement with Russia known as New START. The United States intends to replace the Ohio-class submarines with Columbia-class submarines. These will have sixteen SLBM tubes, which is fewer than the Ohio class. However, the Columbia class are much larger submarines – indeed, they will be the largest submarines the United States has ever built. Building them is the US Navy's top priority, meaning that they will be produced even at the expense of other programs, such as the conventionally armed Virginia-class attack submarines for Australia.

Both classes are supposed to be built at the same shipyards (Groton, Connecticut, and Newport News, Virginia). Since there is a constraint on the US defence industrial base, and the Columbia class ranks higher than the Virginia class, the Columbia-class program gets priority treatment. Australia has committed US$3 billion (A$4.7 billion) to the generic US submarine industrial base, covering both the Virginia and Columbia submarine programs. AUKUS funds will therefore be spent on building a key component of the US nuclear strike force.[17] This fact has not been disclosed to the Australian public or Parliament. Nation-building would imply strengthening our national institutions, such as Parliament, not keeping it in the dark.

Australia may receive its first second-hand Virginia-class submarine in 2033, when the fifth Columbia-class submarine is delivered to the US Navy. Alternatively, Australia may never receive a submarine at all; there is an express provision in the legislation that the United States will not sell a single submarine to Australia unless the US president certifies that doing so would not diminish the underwater capabilities of the US Navy. US production capacity is currently seventeen Virginia-class submarines below the desired number. The US industrial base can produce only 1.2 to 1.4 submarines a year, much lower than the target of 2.33 submarines per year, which is what is needed if Australia is to receive the submarines on time. As such, it is most unlikely that a US president would issue that certification.

The United States also operates nuclear-powered submarines which do not carry ballistic missiles but cruise missiles with conventional, high-explosive, non-nuclear warheads. A cruise missile is self-propelled and self-navigating, and can fly on a flattened, low-altitude trajectory. There have also been submarine-launched cruise missiles that carry a nuclear warhead, but these were withdrawn from service by the US Navy in 1992, after the Cold War ended. The Obama administration retired them in 2013. The Trump administration argued in 2018 that they should be brought back into service. General Mark Milley, then Chairman of the Joint Chiefs of Staff, expressed support for it. There are reports that General Anthony Cotton, the commander of US Strategic Command, has also argued for it.[18] If that happens, then any Virginia-class boats will be equipped with submarine-launched cruise missiles that carry a nuclear warhead. Selling them to Australia would reduce the US fleet. That means either President Trump doesn't mind a reduced fleet, or he does mind, in which case he will not release them to Australia. Australia cannot take possession of those nuclear-armed cruise missile submarines unless it withdraws from the Nuclear Non-Proliferation Treaty.

No boats, no refund?

If Australia does not receive the boats – a realistic possibility – there is no provision in the contract for a refund. A senator from New South Wales, David Shoebridge, asked Vice Admiral Jonathan Mead of the Australian Submarine Agency if there was a refund provision (a 'clawback') in the agreement. It is useful to examine the answers in some detail, so that Australians are fully informed. In the exchange below, taken from *Hansard*, note that Senator Shoebridge's question was about the contents of the existing AUKUS agreement, not a hypothetical question about the future.[19]

Vice Admiral Mead: That's a hypothetical that I'm not going to entertain.

Senator Shoebridge: I'm not asking about a hypothetical; I'm asking about what's in the agreement. It's not a hypothetical. Is there a clawback provision in the agreement?

Vice Admiral Mead: The US has committed to transferring two nuclear powered submarines to Australia.

Senator Shoebridge: ... You know that's not my question. I'm asking: right now, as we sit here, is there a provision in the agreement that we get our money back if the US doesn't live up to its side of the bargain? Surely you included that. Are you telling me you didn't?

Vice Admiral Mead: The US has committed to transferring two nuclear powered submarines and the procurement of a third one.

Senator Shoebridge: So there's no clawback provision.

Vice Admiral Mead: We are investing $3 billion in the US submarine industrial base.

Senator Shoebridge: Whether we get one or not? You cannot be serious.

Vice Admiral Mead: The US has committed to this program.

Patiently, Senator Shoebridge took him through the reasoning, step by step.

> *Senator Shoebridge*: Vice Admiral, you know that the United States legislation provides that the United States can only provide an AUKUS attack class submarine to Australia if, first of all, the US Navy provides an advice that it won't adversely impact their capacity and, secondly, after receipt of that, the President of the United States approves it. You understand that.
>
> *Vice Admiral Mead*: Yes.
>
> *Senator Shoebridge*: If neither of those things happen, we don't get a sub. Do you agree with that?
>
> *Vice Admiral Mead*: I agree with that.
>
> *Senator Shoebridge*: So does the agreement – the one under which we're shelling out $1.5 billion next year, $1.8 billion the year after that and another $1.7 billion, which may be more, over the rest of the decade – provide that, if the United States does not provide us with an AUKUS submarine, we get our money back?
>
> *Vice Admiral Mead*: The US will provide us with an AUKUS submarine.
>
> *Senator Shoebridge*: Did you not understand that my question wasn't about some future hypothetical, about which you would be quite right in taking the point?

I'm asking about what's in the agreement. Is the reason you won't answer what's in the agreement that it embarrassingly fails to have that?

Vice Admiral Mead: You're talking about a future hypothetical.

Senator Shoebridge: I'm talking about what's in the agreement now.

Vice Admiral Mead: The US will provide two submarines and one on procurement.

Senator Shoebridge: I suppose it may be embarrassing that you've entered into an agreement that sees Australian taxpayers shelling out $4.7 billion which we don't get back if we don't get a nuclear sub. That might be embarrassing, but that's not a reason not to answer it. Does the agreement have a clawback provision?

Vice Admiral Mead: I reiterate my statement. The US is committed to transferring two US submarines.

The admiral had praised AUKUS as 'nation-building' and 'the most transformative industrial and technical endeavour in our history'.[20] It is easy to wax lyrical about 'nation-building' when you're talking to compliant journalists. It is quite another thing to encounter genuine questions. The senator asked why there was no provision to get Australia's money back if the United States didn't deliver the submarines: 'Why didn't you do it? Do you have an explanation about why it's not in the agreement?'

> *Vice Admiral Mead*: I just go back to the original statement. The US has committed to providing two US submarines from its submarine industrial base in the early 2030s and a third one on procurement.
>
> *Senator Shoebridge*: And who will the US President be in 2033?
>
> *Vice Admiral Mead*: I do not know.

At this point the admiral was rescued by the Committee chair, Labor Senator Raff Ciccone, who ruled the question 'entirely out of order'. But the point had been made – nobody knows who the US president will be in 2033, or who will be in the US Congress then. There is no provision in the contract to guarantee Australia a refund if the sale doesn't happen. So much for nation-building.

It is also possible that Australia may give up buying nuclear-powered submarines altogether, and opt instead to merely host US submarines in Australia. The Congressional Research Service (CRS) suggested that 'up to eight additional Virginia-class SSNs would be built, and instead of three to five of them being sold to Australia, these additional boats would instead be retained in US Navy service and operated out of Australia'. Australia 'would instead invest those funds in other military capabilities – such as, for example, long-range anti-ship missiles, drones, loitering munitions, B-21 long-range bombers, or other long-range strike aircraft'.[21] Note that 'long-range anti-ship missiles, long-range bombers, and long-range strike aircraft' is code for joining the United States in corralling China inside its own territorial waters in the event of conflict. The CRS canvasses options for the information of the US Congress, not the US president or anyone else in the executive branch of government, but the prospect of such a scenario is quite realistic.

The arrangement may seem strange until you realise that the real rather than declared goal is to demonstrate Australia's relevance to US global supremacy. The declared goal is that Australia will acquire nuclear-powered submarines for 'deterrence'. The real goal is to demonstrate Australia's relevance to the United States as it tries to preserve a US-dominated region. Some submarines may eventually be based in Australia, and may even have Australian flags and personnel, but they will be essentially US boats operated in the United States' great power interests. Sovereignty is more than whose flag is painted on the outside of a boat or who ranks above whom inside it. Sovereignty is about the purpose for which the boats are intended.[22] As former prime minister Scott Morrison said, 'you won't find another defence agreement anywhere in the world where your ally is actually paying to support the industrial base in your own country, in the United States'.[23]

A forward operational deployment of the US Navy

The publicity surrounding AUKUS distracts from perhaps the most important force posture initiative of the United States in the Indo-Pacific – the creation of Submarine Rotation Force-West (SRF-W) at Garden Island, near Fremantle in Western Australia. Australia has committed A$8 billion to upgrade Garden Island's wharves, maintenance facilities and logistics infrastructure. The aim is to increase the number of nuclear-powered attack submarines west of the international date line. By the end of the next decade, there are expected to be twenty-five allied nuclear-powered attack submarines on permanent or rotational deployment in Fremantle, Guam and Hawaii. The spin doctors describe SRF-W as an 'optimal pathway' for AUKUS. In fact, it is a forward operational deployment of the US Navy, independent of AUKUS, not a downpayment on Australia getting its own Virginia-class submarines. In the public's mind, the two are erroneously believed to be the same thing. The boats may never arrive, but SRF-W will remain as a forward operational deployment of the US Navy.

During the Pacific phase of World War II, about 170 Allied submarines were based in that location, with quick access to the Indian Ocean and the Malacca, Lombok and Sunda straits in the archipelago to Australia's north. They were able to cripple enemy shipping. As one analyst notes, 'Those sea lines of communication remain essentially unchanged'.[24] (Sea lines of communication refer to the primary maritime routes for trade, logistics and military operations between ports, not 'communication' in the conversational sense.) SRF-W is a potential threat to China because it can interdict and cripple Chinese energy imports, which must pass through the chokepoint that is the Strait of Malacca after making the long transit across the Indian Ocean. Former president Hu Jintao called it the 'Malacca dilemma' because he recognised that China is vulnerable to having its energy flows choked off there.[25]

SRF-West poses a credible potential threat to China's energy and food security. The base in Western Australia will become one of the most valuable locations for the United States, supporting sustainment, maintenance, repair and mission planning. As Michael McCaul, the chair of the House Foreign Affairs Committee in the US Congress, said, Australia is 'a central base of operations from which to project power'.[26] Australia has thus ensured it is relevant to US military planners. That is the real goal, not nation-building.

Energy and fuel supplies

China's Malacca dilemma should be seen in context. It has been a net oil importer since 1993, and the gap between domestic consumption and domestic production has grown steadily ever since. China had become the largest importer in the world by 2019, relying on imports to meet almost 75 per cent of its consumption. It is also one of the world's largest natural gas importers, relying on imports to meet more than 40 per cent of its domestic needs. It is very vulnerable to being strangled by hostile submarines attacking its shipping.

Australia also needs imports and uses the seas rather than land to transport them. However, fear of being choked off from trade flows has rarely been a realistic concern of Australian policy planners. The Australian Government has examined energy flows carefully. The 2023 *Defence Strategic*

Review described fuel supply as a significant potential vulnerability and called for the creation of a whole-of-government and industry Fuel Council.[27] Here, thanks to the valuable work of former senator Rex Patrick and his Transparency Warrior project, we know that the government, which is keen on AUKUS, doesn't take this pretext seriously.[28] In April 2020, Australia entered into a lease agreement with the United States to store oil in the US Strategic Petroleum Reserve (SPR), on the other side of the Pacific Ocean. That's hardly where Australia's oil reserves ought to be stored, if the government were genuinely worried about being interdicted by an enemy. The government also purchased 1.7 million barrels of oil for storage in the SPR. It sold off this reserve without fanfare in June 2022, leaving Australia with no fuel reserves in the SPR.

Australia's refined fuel comes from Singapore, South Korea, India, Malaysia, Japan and Taiwan. Its crude oil comes from Malaysia, Brunei, Vietnam and the United States. The government doesn't take action to change this import dependence because strangulation is a hollow pretext. Even now, Australia deliberately remains well short of its International Energy Agency obligations to hold ninety days' worth of oil stocks. In January 2025, thanks again to Rex Patrick, the ABC reported that Australia had just twenty-two days' worth of diesel.[29] This is a concern because diesel is a versatile fuel that is used to transport food, equipment and medicines during emergencies, and as a backup fuel to generate electricity for hospitals, water and sanitation, and other critical facilities. In Australia, diesel surpassed electricity as a final consumption fuel about 15 years ago.[30] Claims that nuclear-powered submarines are needed to protect Australia's fuel supplies are not credible. Australian military planners aren't driven by defensive, strangulation scenarios, although they might use them to justify a policy that has other motives.

The last thing China wants is a war in the western Pacific Ocean, which would disrupt nearly all its seaborne supplies. International shipping and air transport companies would rather lose revenue than ships and aircraft, and would stay out of the combat zone – in effect, China would wind up cutting off its own imports. The Australian Government doesn't say openly that it wishes to join the United States in placing China's fuel supplies at risk of interdiction. Perhaps it fears that the public wouldn't support such a goal. It has to portray the policy as defensive, with vague references to fuel supplies being at risk.

A tectonic shift in the alliance

Australia's new and deepening integration into the US war-fighting strategy began with the 2014 Force Posture Agreement between the two countries. That agreement began to rewire Australia's alliance with the United States. The relationship moved to a new level after the 2021 Australia–United States Ministerial Dialogue, where both countries committed to 'enhanced force posture cooperation' between the Australian Defence Force and the US Navy, Marines, Army and Air Force. Both sides also committed to building logistics, sustainment and maintenance facilities 'to support high-end warfighting and combined military operations in the region'. An Australian Defence official described this as a 'tectonic shift' in the alliance. It is an 'historic, albeit largely overlooked' decision, even though the 'transformation has been hiding in plain sight'.[31]

The *New York Times* reported in 2024 that 'an industrial evolution in the American war machine is gathering momentum' in Australia, where ammunition factories are on the verge of producing thousands of artillery shells and guided missiles according to US military specifications. The aim is to replenish US stockpiles, since the ammunition will be produced in partnership with American companies and will be 'no different from those built in the United States'. The reason for production in Australia is obvious – US factories are overstretched by the Ukraine and Gaza conflicts, and the United States cannot produce enough weapons by itself. Australia has an additional opportunity to demonstrate its relevance to US global power. It can become a vital node in a global supply chain. Although the United States has production partnerships with Poland, Japan and India, Australia 'has gone further and faster with the Defense Department and U.S. contractors like Lockheed Martin'.[32]

Manufacturing weapons for the United States is not new; the same places where Australian factories produced weapons during World War II are being revived. In Mulwala, on the Victoria–New South Wales border, weapons factories supported Allied operations in the Pacific during the war. Today, multinational weapons company Thales oversees production in Mulwala and nearby Benalla on a large site with lots of room to expand. The aim is to build a much bigger weapons export industry in Australia under US auspices. The factories will start with relatively simple ammunition such as unguided 155-millimetre artillery shells. Next, Lockheed Martin will begin assembling 'gimmlers', an acronym for Guided Multiple Launch Rocket System (GMLRS). They are designed to be launched from tubes mounted on trucks known as HIMARS, and have been used extensively in Afghanistan and Ukraine. Producing them will give Australian factories the experience needed to make more complex missiles and ammunition.

The *Times* remarks that all this is 'part of an Australian push to essentially become the 51st state for defense production'. Once again, then, we see that the real goal of the project is to demonstrate Australia's relevance to US military planners, not nation-building or 'deterrence'.

Hot-pitting and interoperability

Australian participation is not limited to the undersea domain. It is developing airfields, expanding and strengthening runways for US strategic bombers, building fuel depots, pre-positioning weapons stores and engaging in close cooperation with US airpower as part of an Enhanced Air Cooperation initiative. RAAF Tindal in the Northern Territory will support deployments of up to six B-52 bombers and associated refuelling aircraft. The August 2024 Australia–United States Ministerial Dialogue saw both countries agree to conduct exercises with Japan, which also operates the F-35 Joint Strike Fighter aircraft.[33] That month, three B-2 Spirit heavy strategic stealth bombers deployed to RAAF Amberley in Queensland. They flew thirty-four sorties across southeastern Australia, engaging in joint exercises with Australian fighter aircraft, electronic attack aircraft, aerial refuelling tankers and airborne early warning and control aircraft. They conducted exercises with the RAAF Marine Rotational Force stationed at Darwin, dropping nonexplosive munitions to improve targeting and coordination. They went on to conduct joint training with four Japanese F-35As over the Pacific Ocean for the first time.[34]

The United States also deployed the highly capable F-22 Raptor air superiority fighter aircraft to Australia, where they conducted a joint hot-pit refuel mission with Australia's F-35 aircraft at Curtin airbase in Western Australia. Hot-pit refuelling means that an aircraft will land, refuel and take off without shutting down its engines. Repeated practice allows hot-pitting to be conducted with a smaller number of people and a much smaller logistics footprint. This technique reduces the amount of time needed to respond to a crisis. It also allows the United States to move its jets from one base to another, refuelling as needed, even when no aerial refuelling tanker aircraft are available.

Australia's geography makes it valuable to the United States in the enormous Pacific theatre. Nine thousand kilometres separate Marine Corps Air Station in Miramar, San Diego, from Marine Corps Air Station in Iwakuni, Japan. That is more than twice the distance from Washington to Los Angeles. A RAND Corporation study concluded that the Marine Corps base in Iwakuni, like Kadena Air Base in Okinawa, Japan, can be targeted by China's missile forces.

So can Andersen Air Force Base on Guam.[35] RAAF Base Williamtown, 15 kilometres from the city of Newcastle, New South Wales, allows the US Marine Corps to exercise in Australia. It offers a high level of supply and command-and-control capability. The RAAF operates the land-based F-35A while the Black Knights, a US Marine Corps squadron, operates the land- or aircraft carrier–based F-35C.

A strategic analyst who embedded for a week with the Black Knights observed, 'surrounding any country with permanent and temporary bases that can be used to deny access to sea lanes and launch standoff fire power could reasonably be viewed as provocative'. He added, 'It's equally clear that elements in the Chinese leadership believe US efforts to be tantamount to offensive encirclement – and thus preparation for an unprovoked war'. The 'sheer scale' of the US presence is 'intimidating to any adversary' and 'might prompt worries that the United States intends to strike first'. However, 'Washington pays little regard to these Chinese concerns'.[36] It describes its actions as defensive, and Australia does too, calling them 'integrated deterrence'.

Michael Pezzullo, an Australian strategic analyst and former policy planner, acknowledged that deterrence was a euphemism. 'We're actually so hardwired, in some cases going back decades, into what euphemistically is called US deterrence,' he said.[37] He noted that US forces would not be coming to Australia at the start of a potential crisis with dummy rounds but with their assigned war load. Logically, that would likely include nuclear weapons. He called for a more open discussion with Australians about the implications.

Australian policy planners know that Australia could become a target if key US assets are stationed here – but that is not their greatest concern. Rather, they strive to show their relevance to American policy-makers precisely because they know how little Australia features in US thinking. The more vulnerable the United States becomes in Japan, Taiwan and the northern Philippines, the more attractive Australia becomes as a secure location for US forces. Australia's geography is also convenient for US space ambitions. Clear skies and low levels of cloud cover provide an advantage in the optical and optical-hybrid communications systems markets. Australia hosts the C-band space surveillance radar and the space surveillance telescope. The Australian continent covers one-third of the Earth's rotation. We look directly into the solar system, unlike countries in the northern hemisphere. That makes us valuable for deep space communications systems. Australia will develop launch capability for equatorial- and polar-orbiting satellites, benefiting from vast coastlines, open water and stable weather.[38] The buildup ensures that the United States pays greater attention to Australia, in its own self-interest.

Dominance as deterrence

There are good reasons for Australia to modernise its submarine fleet. Nation-building would not be harmed if Australia bought Air-Independent Propulsion submarines and the suite of equipment mentioned earlier. They make the most sense on grounds of performance, defence relevance, cost and non-proliferation. The obvious question left, then, is why such determination to acquire nuclear-powered submarines? Nation-building isn't a credible answer. Nor are other, defensive or benign-sounding terms, such as 'deterrence' and 'a favourable balance of power'.[39] The answer is what it has been since the United States became the leading superpower after World War II – military dominance, also known as 'preponderant power'. 'Preponderant power must be the objective of U.S. policy', as a crucial US National Security Memorandum stated in 1952, and 'preponderant power' remains its objective today.[40]

Australia will demonstrate its relevance to this core US objective. AUKUS thus fits comfortably into the trajectory of Australian defence policy. The Royal Australian Navy did not try to develop a balanced force in the years after World War II. Instead, it focused on anti-submarine warfare to support US naval strategy. Australia converted Q-class destroyers to Q-class anti-submarine frigates in the 1950s. It conducted comprehensive research on anti-submarine warfare technology, producing the Ikara long-range anti-submarine guided missile, the Mulloka sonar and the Barra sonobuoy. The aircraft carrier HMAS *Melbourne* used Fairey Gannet and Grumman Tracker aircraft and Westland Wessex and Westland Sea King helicopters in the anti-submarine role. The idea, then and now, was interoperability – operating inside the strategy of a superpower by contributing a well-chosen, niche capability to augment the larger force.[41]

Interoperability is central to the Australian way of war. When Defence Minister Richard Marles talks up the importance of interoperability and interchangeability with the US Navy and the Royal Navy, he is well within the mainstream of Australian military strategy. There is nothing new about a system in which the imperial power provides global maritime supremacy, sub-imperial powers such as Australia contribute forces as needed, and the entire imperial system cooperates during a general war or a major international crisis. This system used to be called Imperial Defence. As the Minister for Defence, Joseph Cook, told Parliament in 1909: 'We must remember, first of all, that Australia is part of the Empire, and that within our means we must recognise both our Imperial and local responsibilities. The Empire floats upon its fleet. A strong fleet means a strong Empire, and therefore it is our duty to add to the fleet strength of the Empire.'[42]

Cook could have been speaking about AUKUS in 2025, apart from the word 'empire', which has its own euphemism today – a 'rules-based international order'.[43] Australia's purchase of nuclear-powered submarines, along with many other aspects of its defence and foreign relations, is designed to show its commitment to defending a US-led order. AUKUS is intended to demonstrate Australia's relevance to this goal. The doctrinally approved term is 'deterrence', not 'dominance'. It is more in line with contemporary sentiments. But, from a military perspective, the idea is not new: put your bases on the edge of enemy territory, and patrol as far forward as possible. The military purpose is recognisably MacArthur's. The public may support the real goal – demonstrating Australia's relevance to the United States as it tries to dominate China – but that question has not been put to the public in a meaningful way.

The strategic logic of AUKUS is to demonstrate Australia's relevance to the US goal of 'dominance'.

6

Turbulence

WHAT IS THE UNITED States trying to achieve in the second Trump administration? What are the geopolitical implications for Australia and the world? *Turbulence* shows that Donald Trump wants US global primacy over China. If he cannot control it, he wants economic separation from it. AUKUS is not an investment in nation-building, despite ideologically strident claims by Australia's leaders. It is a contribution of people, territory, materials, money, diplomacy and ideology to the war-fighting capabilities of the United States. 'Deterrence' does have a non-ideological, defensive meaning but in this case it is a euphemism for 'dominance'. The Australian public may support these goals, but they have not been asked about them in a meaningful way, nor have they been told there are viable alternatives.[1] Perhaps they haven't been asked because their elected leaders fear the answer.

How all this will unfold is unclear, but a few observations are in order. First and foremost, seen in a wider context, Trump's vision is escapism of a backward-looking kind, the very kind that might make you feel you're at the Hotel California, trying to find your way back to old times that may or may not have existed.[2] His talk of 'revitalizing the domestic steel and aluminum industries'[3] harks back to the world of the 1950s, when he was a teenager, US economic and military power dominated much of the world, and presidents didn't worry about climate change, environmental pollution, or the demands of feminists and minority groups. His financial and legal coercion of universities is an attempt to recreate the docility and conformity of 1950s culture. Universities were willing servants of government and corporate power. They encouraged patriotic ideology, the glorification of US corporations, the militarisation of US society, and the repression of popular movements abroad ('counterinsurgency').[4] The politicisation of higher education in those years was so profound that it was assumed to be the natural order of things, so much so that democratic challenges from a younger generation were condemned as a 'crisis of democracy'.[5]

Make America Great Again nostalgia is a fearful response to the present. It is the opposite of the forward-looking US optimism exemplified by Ralph Waldo Emerson: 'I simply experiment, an endless seeker with no Past at my back'.[6] Graham Fuller, the CIA's former head of long-range strategic forecasting, said in 2023 that the United States has 'adopted what can only be described as a fundamentally negative geopolitical vision: do what it takes to block Chinese and Russian influence in the world in a desperate attempt to prove that we can still call the shots'. President Biden's policies had a similar vision; Fuller writes that the number of countries with which the United States refused to seriously engage grew ever larger, even as China declared its 'willingness to do business with all countries where mutual benefits are to be gained'.[7]

Trump's vision will face a combination of resistance and acquiescence. Despite the global upheavals caused by his barrage of tariffs, the US economy remains as powerful and alluring to foreign investors as ever. Soon after the tariffs were imposed in March and April 2025, AustralianSuper, Australia's largest superannuation fund, said it would continue to invest more than half its A$367 billion in assets in the United States. Mark Delaney, its chief investment officer, informed the *Financial Times* that 'strong productivity growth, strong profit growth and, by any measure, many of the best companies in the world' made the United States 'an attractive place to store capital'. The tariffs were a 'significant volatility event' but they wouldn't change the fund's exposure in the United States.[8]

Australia's foreign and defence policies remain resolutely sub-imperial: attempting to preserve dominance over the southwest Pacific and smaller neighbours in Southeast Asia such as Timor-Leste while demonstrating relevance to US global primacy through AUKUS.[9] The declared goals are 'deterrence' and 'freedom of navigation'. The real goals were expressed candidly by Douglas MacArthur: 'we can dominate with sea and air power every Asiatic port from Vladivostok to Singapore'.[10]

The cloak of 'freedom of navigation' hides the nature and purpose of Australia's military operations from the public. It protects the government from democratic accountability, and from debate on the priorities of Australia's intelligence agencies and the Australian Defence Force. Concealing the real rather than declared goals of the policy is not national security in any meaningful sense. These are questions for democratic debate. They do not require the disclosure of intelligence information or operationally sensitive tactics.

The contrast between Australia's real rather than declared goals was evident in one of Australia's longest military commitments – the twenty-year presence in Afghanistan. The real goal wasn't reconstructing Afghanistan or promoting feminism or other pretexts but demonstrating Australia's relevance to the United States. Years after he left office, Joel Fitzgibbon, Australia's Defence Minister from 2007 to 2009, said that 'from an Australian government perspective, we were really only there out of alliance commitment. I had a realisation we were just marking time [in Afghanistan]. The boys [soldiers] weren't, but as a government we were.' His remarks offer a valuable insight into policy-makers' ability to believe what they need to believe to defend the policy: 'When I stood up in parliament and said positive things about what we were doing, I meant it. You have to believe it. Was there scepticism in the back of my mind? Yes, there was.'[11] Australia's long presence in Afghanistan was tied to the US presence there.[12] Australia didn't withdraw its troops until the United States did. Demonstrating relevance was the real rather than the declared policy objective.

The media generally followed the flag, reporting government claims in a sympathetic manner. Australians were reassured that the 'targeting process has an ever-growing number of checks and balances ... from the smallest Australian commando operation, through to the highly secretive US squads, their commanders are watching. "They are f---ing on their shoulder, every f---ing day and every f---ing night," one soldier says.'[13] The costs were measured in terms of Australian blood and treasure, not the lives of ordinary people in Afghanistan, many of whom were killed or maimed while merely attending weddings or engaging in agriculture. There is no evidence that AUKUS reflects a different moral calculus – by the government or the media.

True believers in AUKUS are just one generation removed from true believers in the Afghanistan commitment. Some individuals belong to both categories. The pattern is familiar. Just as 'experts' in counterinsurgency enjoyed media opportunities to advocate for remaining in Afghanistan, a new set of experts is now at hand to advocate for AUKUS. Their expertise is worth taking seriously on questions of ship knowledge, navigation, seamanship and ship handling. But the desired objective of Australia's defence policy is a question of politics, not technical expertise. There is no reason to defer to 'experts' on fundamental political questions – should Australia focus on demonstrating relevance to the United States or some other, more independent aim?

Challenges to Trump's plans are visible on the horizon. Europe's advanced industrial powers (Germany, France, the Netherlands) may not indefinitely obey US orders to abandon the huge, lucrative Chinese market. They may not indefinitely accept decline or deindustrialisation. Asian governments may be ambivalent about the growing power of China, and many may deeply distrust it – but that does not imply that they want to accept a US-imposed future. The desire for some form of Asian regionalism has deep historical roots.[14] Change may come in the Middle East, too. It has the largest youth cohort in the world, with 60 per cent of the population under the age of thirty.[15] It also has the highest youth unemployment rate in the world. Authoritarian Arab states have failed to deliver for their people, despite their oil and gas riches. They have not kept pace with the more dynamic northeast Asian economies; Egypt's and South Korea's economies were roughly similar in 1960. Today, Egypt's economy is more than four times smaller, but its population is twice the size of South Korea's.[16] China's outreach to the Middle East, offering infrastructure, finance and training, may be alluring.

It remains to be seen what effect Israel's military operations in the Occupied Palestinian Territories will have on the young Arab population. Some may well wonder why their leaders spent billions buying advanced US weaponry but had no intention or ability to impose a no-fly zone to protect Palestinian civilians. Or why South Africa, and not an Arab government, took action at the International Court of Justice in support of the Palestinians. There may be geopolitical consequences in the years ahead, if history is a guide. More than fifty years ago, the scholar-activist Ruth First distinguished between anti-democratic coups by army generals and 'the Coup of the Young Majors', which were modernising moves against stagnant, traditional elites and politically backward military rulers.[17] The Arab defeats to Israel in 1948 were followed four years later by a wave of decolonial revolutions in the Arab world. Egypt was the first to move, with a revolution in 1952 that saw the overthrow of King Farouk by the Free Officers Movement. Similar developments occurred in Syria and Iraq (1958), Algeria and North Yemen (1962) and Sudan and Libya (1969). Junior- and middle-ranking officers in the Arab world today may well be at the head of similar events in years to come. As Zleekhah Mohtaseb, a Palestinian tour guide and translator, said, 'Every person in the world dreams to be free'.[18] If so, authoritarian rulers in the Arab world may be supported by their own intelligence agencies, Israeli surveillance technology, and covert and overt Western power.

Demographic change occurs in Australia, too. From the late eighteenth century until the early twenty-first century, Australia remained the second most English country in the world. At Federation in 1901, Australians were almost exclusively British: as many as one in five had been born in the British Isles, and almost everyone else was descended from British or Irish immigrants.[19] But Australia is increasingly a multi-origin society now. That means recognising the way domestic politics relates to foreign policy. The government has hit upon 'social cohesion' as its preferred way of handling public opposition. But calls for social cohesion cannot be indifferent to a dynamic in which one group of Australians regularly sends members of its community to serve as occupation forces, prison guards or spies against the relatives of another group of Australians. This would be true of Australians from the Balkans, the Middle East, the Indian subcontinent, the African continent, South America,[20] or Timor-Leste.[21] Contemporary events in the Occupied Palestinian Territories may result in domestic constituencies mobilising around this issue.

All this is unlikely to go uncontested, and may be just a mild foretaste of what is yet to come in the event of a conflict involving China. The social fractures in Australia would be significant. 'Social cohesion' programs may not suffice to heal them. AUKUS signifies a commitment to a world order that Australia's planners would like to see, not one that is actually emerging. If faith collides with reality, reality will win. It always does.

Acknowledgements

I am grateful to UNSW Canberra for an atmosphere conducive to research. I acknowledge many individuals on campus:

At the Academy Library: Michael Lemmer, Anna Papoulis, Deborah Despard, Erin Wishart, Susan Powter, Jacques Montagner, Owen Litchfield, Anna Gabriel, Jamie Redmond, Felicita Carr, Katherine Burton, Semra Griffiths, Jonathon Guppy and Annette McGuiness. In the Learning and Teaching Group: Emma Betts, Emily Rutherford, Anne Lahey, Fadhila Pratiwi, Janene Harman, Marty Jones and Bhavani Kannan. In the Creative and Print Unit: Barry Freebody, John Carroll and Jeffrey Steinacker. The Future Operations Research Group at UNSW Canberra, especially David Kilcullen. The Naval Studies Group at UNSW Canberra, especially the late James Goldrick AO, CSC RAN. The UNSW Canberra Space program, especially Andrew Lambert (now working in industry). My colleagues in the School of Humanities and Social Sciences, headed by Craig Stockings, and especially the Administration and Support Team: Tammy Hayes, John

Maughan, Maher Aladdin, Lisa Goese, Brodie Gibson. My colleagues in the Indo-Pacific Studies program, 2025: David Lee, Kirstie Petrou, Heather Neilson, Douglas Guilfoyle, Fiona Allen, Minako Sakai, Nicolaas Warouw. My colleagues in the International and Political Studies program, 2025. The Chief of Air Force Air and Space Power Fellow, Wing Commander Lewis Frederickson. Former Director of War Studies, Australian Army Research Centre, Professor Albert Palazzo. The Chief of Army Military Fellow, Lieutenant Colonel (retd) Leo Purdy.

I am grateful to the Arena Publications team for the opportunity to develop some of the ideas in this book. Its core arguments were presented at an Arena Conjuncture event, 'If we make it through November…' on 11 October 2024 in Loft Two, 49 Smith Street, Collingwood. I thank Alison Caddick, John Hinkson, Simon Cooper, Timothy Ström, Guy Rundle, Paul James and Julia Cretan.

I thank Patrick O'Neil for commissioning an opinion piece for *The Age* in February 2025. My interactions with him informed the structure of this book. I thank the editor of *Australian Book Review*, Georgina Arnott, and the editor emeritus, Peter Rose, for the opportunity to review publications that informed *Turbulence*.

I also thank Nathan Hollier, Maher Mughrabi, Matthew Burr, Brendan Thorne, Adam Smith, Mark Horvath, Jeff Morgan and Mark Stone for productive discussions.

I am grateful to the *Bulletin of the Atomic Scientists* for providing the public, policy-makers and scientists with critical information. Likewise, the Federation of American

Scientists, especially the Nuclear Information Project: Hans M Kristensen, Matt Korda, Eliana Johns and Mackenzie Knight-Boyle. For similar reasons, the Union of Concerned Scientists and the Arms Control Association.

I thank Klaus Dodds for introducing me to his field of Geopolitics. I thank Paul Daley for his encouragement and thoughtfulness.

I thank Robert Redwine, Barry Pozen, Jolyon Howorth, Michael Pettis, Richard Kozul-Wright, Andrew Serdy, Drew Christiansen S.J., Robert Buzzanco and Michael Leach.

Journalist and radio host Doug Henwood's *Behind the News* program has been a useful companion for several years.

I thank the staff at Melbourne University Publishing: Foong Ling Kong, Duncan Fardon, Cathryn Smith, Kate Mahoney and Holly Hendry-Saunders. They even came up with the title when I couldn't. I thank John Mapps for his copyediting of this manuscript and Sherrey Quinn for the index.

I am grateful to Ian Latham, barrister, for his ongoing support.

I thank Margaret Douglas for her support.

For their generosity and valuable suggestions, I am grateful to Philip Dorling, Scott Burchill, Rex Patrick, Davy Fernandes, Derek Fernandes and Deb Salvagno.

Noam Chomsky suggested that it would be necessary to undertake a course of intellectual self-defence to lay the basis for more meaningful democracy, and to protect ourselves from manipulation and control. *Turbulence* is motivated by this suggestion.

The usual disclaimers apply.

Notes

1 Janan Ganesh, 'The hopeless search for Trump's cunning plan', *Financial Times*, 9 April 2025.
2 Damien Cave, 'Australia may well be the world's most secretive democracy', *New York Times*, 5 June 2019.

1 'WE'LL GET RICHER IF HE WINS': THE TRUMP AGENDA AT HOME AND ABROAD

1 '"We'll get richer if he wins": Wall Street goes Maga', *Financial Times*, Due Diligence Newsletter, 30 May 2024.
2 Peter Charalambous, Laura Romero and Soo Rin Kim, 'Trump has tapped an unprecedented 13 billionaires for his administration', American Broadcasting Company (ABCNews), 18 December 2024.
3 Amanda Gordon and Sridhar Natarajan, 'Wall Street billionaires are rushing to back Trump, verdict be damned', Bloomberg, 31 May 2024.
4 Thomas Ferguson, *Golden Rule: The Investment Theory of Party Competition and the Logic of Money-Driven Political Systems*, University of Chicago Press, 1995.
5 Amelia McGuire, 'The top five billionaire tech bros who are on the Trump train', *Australian Financial Review*, 5 November 2024.

6 Brooke Harrington, 'The broligarchs are trying to have their way', *The Atlantic*, 4 August 2024.

7 Thomas Ferguson, Paul Jorgensen and Jie Chen, 'Industrial structure and party competition in an age of Hunger Games: Donald Trump and the 2016 presidential election', 1 February 2018, Institute for New Economic Thinking Working Paper Series No. 66.

8 Jacob Bogage, 'The national debt is ballooning. The next president probably won't stop it', *Washington Post*, 24 June 2024.

9 Alan Blinder, 'Almost everything is wrong with the new tax law', *Wall Street Journal*, 27 December 2017.

10 The Ethics Centre, 'Ethics Explainer: Social license to operate', 23 January 2018.

11 Quinn Slobodian, *Hayek's Bastards: Race, Gold, IQ, and the Capitalism of the Far Right*, Princeton University Press, 2025. For an antidote, see Ned Block, 'How heritability misleads about race', *Cognition*, vol. 56, issue 2, August 1995, 99–128; Noam Chomsky, 'Equality: Language development, human intelligence, and social organization', in *The Chomsky Reader*, James Peck (ed.), Pantheon Books, 1987, 195–9.

12 SM Amadae, *Prisoners of Reason: Game Theory and Neoliberal Political Economy*, Cambridge University Press, 2016; Nancy MacLean, *Democracy in Chains: The Deep History of the Radical Right's Stealth Plan for America*, Viking, 2017.

13 Face the Nation transcript, 23 August 2015: Trump, Christie & Cruz, CBS News.

14 Alan Rappeport, 'Trump promised to kill carried interest. Lobbyists kept it alive', *New York Times*, 22 December 2017.

15 Eliot Brown, 'Carried interest tax rate comes under fire, again, from Trump', *Wall Street Journal*, 7 February 2025.

16 Jennifer Mittelstadt, 'Why does Trump threaten America's allies? Hint: It starts in 1919', *New York Times*, 2 February 2025.

17 The White House, 'Addressing egregious actions of the Republic of South Africa', 7 February 2025.

18 Chris McGreal, 'How the roots of the "PayPal mafia" extend to apartheid South Africa', *Guardian*, 27 January 2025; Chris McGreal, '"White supremacists in suits and ties": The right-wing Afrikaner group in Trump's ear', *Guardian*, 14 February 2025.
19 Jim Tankersley, Emma Bubola, Andrew Higgins and Aurelien Breeden, 'Trump is leading a global surge to the right', *New York Times*, 23 January 2025.
20 Flavia Krause-Jackson, 'The three women who want to reshape the European Union', Bloomberg, 4 April 2025.
21 Josh Dawsey, Vera Bergengruen and Alexander Ward, 'The painting that explains Trump's foreign policy', *Wall Street Journal*, 13 March 2025; Hampton Sides, *Blood and Thunder: An Epic of the American West*, Doubleday, 2006.
22 The White House, 'Inaugural address', 20 January 2025.
23 Niall Ferguson, *Colossus: The Rise and Fall of the American Empire*, Penguin, 2012; RW Van Alstyne, *The Rising American Empire*, Oxford University Press, 1960, 35.
24 Elbridge Colby, *The Strategy of Denial: American Defense in an Age of Great Power Conflict*, Yale University Press, 2021, 21.
25 Leonard W Levy, *Emergence of a Free Press*, Oxford University Press, 1985, 16.
26 *New York Times Co. v. Sullivan*, 376 US 254 (1964).
27 Lawrence Friedman, *Inventors of the Promised Land*, Knopf, 1975, 44–78.
28 Noam Chomsky, *Rethinking Camelot: JFK, the Vietnam War, and U.S. Political Culture*, Verso, 1993.
29 Martin and Annelise Anderson, *Reagan's Secret War*, Crown Publishers, 2009, 395.
30 Elizabeth Dias, 'Christianity will have power', *New York Times*, 9 August 2020.
31 *Kennedy v. Bremerton School District*, 597 US, No. 21-418 (2022); *Lemon v. Kurtzman*, 403 US 602 (1971).
32 Daniel A Cox, 'After the ballots are counted', Survey Center on American Life, 11 February 2021.

33 Public Religion Research Institute, 'The American religious landscape in 2023, 29 August 2024'; Public Religion Research Institute, 'Religion and the 2024 presidential election', 8 November 2024.
34 Elizabeth Dias and Ruth Graham, 'Trump's believers see a presidency with god on their side', *New York Times*, 7 November 2024.
35 Elizabeth Dias and Ruth Graham, 'Southern Baptists move to purge churches with female pastors', *New York Times*, 13 June 2023.
36 Larry M Bartels, *Unequal Democracy: The Political Economy of the New Gilded Age,* 2nd ed., Princeton University Press, 2018; Benjamin I Page and Martin Gilens, *Democracy in America? What Has Gone Wrong and What We Can Do About It*, University of Chicago Press, 2020.
37 Shelby Talcott, '"A dying empire led by bad people": Poll finds young voters despairing over US politics', *Semafor*, 29 May 2024.
38 Anthony Capaccio and Courtney McBride, 'Trump's "Golden Dome" system spurs flood of defense industry pitches', Bloomberg, 14 March 2025.
39 Mariana Mazzucato, *The Entrepreneurial State*, Anthem Press, 2013.
40 Walter Isaacson, *Steve Jobs: The Exclusive Biography*, Abacus, 2015.
41 Siladitya Ray, 'Trump hails "super genius" Elon Musk in victory speech', *Forbes*, 6 November 2024.
42 Desmond Butler, Trisha Thadani, Emmanuel Martinez, Aaron Gregg, Luis Melgar, Jonathan O'Connell and Dan Keating, 'Elon Musk's business empire is built on $38 billion in government funding', *Washington Post*, 26 February 2025.
43 'Shall we have airplanes?', *Fortune*, January 1948, 77.
44 Frank Kofsky, *Harry S. Truman and the War Scare of 1948: A Successful Campaign to Deceive the Nation*, St Martin's, 1993, 37.
45 Kofsky, *Harry S. Truman and the War Scare of 1948*, 48, 81, 319 n.7; *Businessweek*, 'Finance: War baby in a peace economy', 7 June 1947, 58–63.

46 National Air and Space Museum, 'Commercial aviation at mid-century', airandspace.si.edu.
47 Laura D'Andrea Tyson, *Who's Bashing Whom? Trade Conflict in High-Technology Industries*, Institute for International Economics, 1992, 88–90.
48 Winfried Ruigrock and Rob Van Tulder, *The Logic of International Restructuring*, Routledge, 1995, 220–21.
49 Robert Reich, 'High Tech, a subsidiary of Pentagon Inc.', *New York Times*, 29 May 1985, A23.
50 Michael Schmidt, 'As election nears, Kelly warns Trump would rule like a dictator', *New York Times*, 22 October 2024.
51 Gabe Whisnant and Jesus Mesa, 'Donald Trump wants to "get rid" of nuclear weapons', *Newsweek*, 6 March 2025.
52 *Businessweek*, 'From Cold War to Cold Peace', no. 1015, 12 February 1949, 19–20.
53 Jimmy Goodrich, 'Don't be fooled, advanced chips are important for national security', RAND Corporation, 10 February 2025.
54 Benn Steil, *The Battle of Bretton Woods: John Maynard Keynes, Harry Dexter White, and the Making of a New World Order*, Princeton University Press, 2013, 125.
55 Statement by Henry Morgenthau Jr (Washington, 7 March 1945), www.cvce.eu.
56 Hugh Dalton, *Hansard* (UK), Commons Chamber, vol. 436, 15 April 1947.
57 Jay Surti, 'Back to basics: Risk and return: The search for yield', International Monetary Fund Communications Department, vol. 58, issue 002, June 2021, 48–9.
58 Christopher Leonard, *The Lords of Easy Money*, Simon & Schuster, 2023.
59 Donald Trump, Inaugural Address, 20 January 2017, trumpwhitehouse.archives.gov.
60 Andrew Rosenthal, 'Trump gives us "American Carnage"', *New York Times*, 20 January 2017; Ben Domenech, 'The "Dark Knight" inauguration', *New York Times*, 21 January 2017.

61 Anne Case and Angus Deaton, 'Rising morbidity and mortality in midlife among white non-Hispanic Americans in the 21st century', *PNAS,* vol. 112, no. 49, 8 December 2015, 15078–83.
62 Patrick Ruffini, 'The emerging working-class Republican majority', *Politico*, 4 November 2023.
63 'Remarks by President Biden at a Campaign Reception', 20 October 2023, www.whitehouse.gov.

2 FRONTLINE EUROPE

1 CNN, Donald Trump Interview on Larry King Live, 2 September 1987.
2 Donald Trump, 'An open letter from Donald J. Trump on why America should stop paying to defend countries that can afford to defend themselves', *New York Times*, 2 September 1987, A28.
3 Marc Fisher, 'Over four decades, Trump's one solid stance: A hard line on trade', *Washington Post*, 8 March 2018.
4 Hedrick Smith, 'Reagan is promising a crusade to make nation great again', *New York Times*, 15 July 1980.
5 David M Kennedy and Thomas Bailey, *The American Spirit: United States History as Seen by Contemporaries, Vol 1: to 1877*, Wadsworth Cengage Learning, 2009, 276.
6 Cary T Grayson, Diary, 10 March 1919, Woodrow Wilson Presidential Library, Staunton, Virginia, Identifier: WWP17100.
7 David Montgomery, *The Fall of the House of Labor*, Cambridge University Press, 1987, 464.
8 David Ellwood, *Italy 1943–1945*, Leicester University Press, 1985, 157.
9 Gabriel Kolko, *The Politics of War*, Pantheon, 1990, 43–63, 172–93, 428–56, 616–26.
10 Charles Cabell (CIA deputy director), cited in National Security Archive, 'CIA releases controversial Bay of Pigs history', 2016, Document 05 ('Evolution of CIA's Anti-Castro Policies,

1951–January 1961'), 27. See also Wayne Smith, *The Closest of Enemies*, Norton, 1987.

11 Office of the Historian, *Foreign Relations of the United States, 1961–1963, Volume XII: American Republics*, Document 7 (10 March 1961), US Department of State, 1996.

12 Richard Welch, *Response to Revolution*, University of North Carolina Press, 1985, 18.

13 Peo Hansen and Stefan Jonsson, *Eurafrica: The Untold History of European Integration and Colonialism*, Bloomsbury, 2014.

14 Bernard Fall, *Street without Joy: The French Debacle in Indochina*, Stackpole Books, 1961; Ngo Vinh Long, *Before the Revolution: The Vietnamese Peasants Under the French*, Columbia University Press, 1991.

15 Megan Brown, *The Seventh Member State*, Harvard University Press, 2022, 167.

16 Hans Kundnani, *Eurowhiteness*, Hurst, 2023, 2, 65–6.

17 Office of the Historian, *Foreign Relations of the United States, 1948, Volume I, Part 2: General; The United Nations*, Document 4, US Department of State, 1976.

18 Matina Stevis-Gridneff, 'Crude comments from Europe's top diplomat point to bigger problems', *New York Times*, 17 October 2022.

19 Kundnani, *Eurowhiteness*, 115.

20 Maia de la Baume, 'MEPs approve Schinas despite "protecting European way of life" controversy', *Politico*, 4 October 2019.

21 Anderw Stroehlein, 'Europe's "let them die" policy', Human Rights Watch, 14 September 2022.

22 People's Republic of China, 'A global community of shared future, Belt and Road Forum', September 2023, www.beltandroadforum.org.

23 Alan S Blinder and Mark Zandi, 'The financial crisis: Lessons for the next one', Center on Budget and Policy Priorities, 15 October 2015.

24 Wayne Swan, *The Good Fight*, Allen & Unwin, 2014.

25 Jeremy Shapiro and Jana Puglierin, 'The art of vassalisation', *ECFR Policy Brief*, April 2023.
26 Tom Fairless and David Luhnow, 'The tech industry is huge – and Europe's share of it is very small', *Wall Street Journal*, 19 May 2025.
27 Felix Richter, 'Big Tech v Europe: Overseas dominance', *Statista*, 26 November 2021.
28 John Mickelthwait and Adrian Wooldridge, 'For Europe, the next US president is a shock – and a catalyst for change', Bloomberg, 13 November 2024.
29 *Times Higher Education*, World University Rankings 2025.
30 Gideon Rachman, 'Europe has fallen behind America and the gap is growing', *Financial Times*, 20 June 2023.
31 Brendan Simms, *Europe: The Struggle for Supremacy, 1453 to the Present*, Allen Lane, 2013, 243.
32 Hans Kundnani, *The Paradox of German Power*, Oxford University Press, 2014, 7–22.
33 Marco D'Eramo, 'Sinking Germany', Sidecar, *New Left Review*, 19 July 2022.
34 Andreas Rinke, Victoria Waldersee and Sarah Marsh, 'German business chiefs clash with Berlin over China policies', Reuters, 14 October 2022.
35 Javier Blas, 'Europe's petrochemical industry is heading for Death Row', Bloomberg, 20 November 2023.
36 Brooke Masters, 'Energy crisis gives US chance to woo big European companies', *Financial Times*, 1 November 2022.
37 Mario Draghi, 'The future of European competitiveness', European Commission, September 2024.
38 James K Galbraith, 'The gift of sanctions: An analysis of assessments of the Russian economy, 2022–2023', Institute for New Economic Thinking Working Paper Series No. 204 (10 April 2023).
39 Anu Bradford, *The Brussels Effect*, Oxford University Press, 2020.

40 Anu Bradford, *Digital Empires*, Oxford University Press, 2023.
41 Steven Erlanger, 'Trump weakens the Brussels Effect', *New York Times*, 27 February 2025.
42 David Brennan, 'Donald Trump says EU set up to hurt US', *Newsweek*, 27 November 2018.
43 Bob Davis, 'Interview with President Trump', *Wall Street Journal*, 26 November 2018.
44 Steven Erlanger, 'Indifference or hostility? Trump's view of European allies raises alarm', *New York Times*, 27 February 2025.
45 Alexander Brzozowski, 'US ambassador: Europe should forget Huawei, embrace Western tech', *Globsec 2019 Event Report – Navigating through the EU's Uncertain Waters*, June 2019.
46 David M Herszenhorn, 'Trump's man in Brussels slams "out of touch" EU', *Politico Europe*, 10 December 2018.
47 Brzozowski, 'US ambassador: Europe should forget Huawei, embrace Western tech'.
48 Geir Lundestad, *The United States and Western Europe*, Oxford University Press, 2003, 27–31.
49 Linde Desmaele, 'Unpacking the Trump administration's grand strategy in Europe', *European Security*, vol. 31, no. 2, 2022, 180–99.
50 David Sanger, 'Europe's new reality: Trump may not quit NATO, but he's already undercutting it', *New York Times*, 20 February 2025.
51 Andrew Small, 'Transatlantic cooperation on Asia and the Trump administration', German Marshall Fund, 2019.
52 Steven Erlanger, 'Europe vows to spend more on defense, but US still isn't happy', *New York Times*, 6 June 2019.
53 Aaron Mehta, 'US warns against "protectionism" with new EU defense agreement', *Defense News*, 15 February 2018.
54 Alexander Brzozowski, *Globsec 2019 Event Report – Navigating through the EU's Uncertain Waters*, June 2019.
55 Peter Hennessy and James Jinks, *The Silent Deep: The Royal Navy Submarine Service Since 1945*, Penguin, 2015, 243.

56 Hans M Kristensen, Matt Korda, Eliana Johns and Mackenzie Knight, 'United Kingdom nuclear weapons', 2024, *Bulletin of the Atomic Scientists*, vol. 80, no. 6, 394–407; Daniel Michaels, Noemie Bisserbe and Michael R Gordon, 'Trump prompts European calls for a homegrown nuclear umbrella', *Wall Street Journal*, 24 March 2025.

57 Laura Kayali, Thorsten Jungholt and Philipp Fritz, 'Europe is quietly debating a nuclear future without the US', *Politico*, 7 April 2024.

58 Max Bergmann and Sophia Besch, 'Why European defense still depends on America', *Foreign Affairs*, 7 March 2023.

59 Jean-Pierre Maulny, 'Takuba Task Force: A new approach to European military cooperation?', *Ad-Hoc European Military Cooperation Outside Europe*, Ed Arnold (ed.), RUSI Occasional Paper, December 2021, 3–10.

60 Alexandr Burilkov and Guntram B Wolff, 'Defending Europe without the US', *Bruegel*, 21 February 2025.

61 NATO, 'Defence expenditure of NATO countries (2014–2024)', June 2024.

62 Burilkov and Wolff, 'Defending Europe without the US'.

63 Alex Horton and Hannah Natanson, 'Secret Pentagon memo on China, homeland has Heritage fingerprints', *Washington Post*, 30 March 2025.

3 FRONTLINE MIDDLE EAST

1 Adam Taylor, John Hudson and Hajar Harb, 'Blinken presses Israel's Netanyahu on dire conditions in northern Gaza', *Washington Post*, 22 October 2024.

2 Daniel Estrin and Aya Batrawy, 'Israel threatens to starve out northern Gaza, UN aid agencies say', NPR, 15 October 2024.

3 Steve Hendrix and Hazem Balousha, 'Israeli siege plan for Gaza under scrutiny as US demands urgent change', *Washington Post*, 16 October 2024.

4 DFAT, 'Joint statement to the UN Third Committee', 22 October 2024.
5 DFAT, 'Humanitarian Situation in Gaza', 3 June 2024.
6 Alex McKinnon, 'From "deep" to "grave" on the Gaza concern-o-meter', Everything is Fine, 16 February 2024.
7 Alex McKinnon, 'How Fatima Payman killed change from within', Everything is Fine, 1 July 2024.
8 David Reynolds, *The Long Shadow: Legacies of the Great War in the 20th Century*, Norton, 2014, 66.
9 VH Rothwell, 'Mesopotamia in British war aims, 1914–1918', *The Historical Journal*, vol. 13, no. 2, June 1970, 273–94.
10 Ian Rutledge, *Addicted to Oil*, I.B. Tauris, 2005, 25.
11 Office of the Historian, *Foreign Relations of the United States, Diplomatic Papers, 1943, Volume IV: The Near East and Africa*, Document 1006 (13 November 1943), Department of State, 1964.
12 Office of the Historian, *Foreign Relations of the United States, Diplomatic Papers, 1943, Volume IV: The Near East and Africa*, Memorandum to the Secretary of State (9 October 1945), Department of State, 1964.
13 Arathy Somasekhar and Noah Browning, 'US refiners step up imports of gasoline-friendly West African crude', Reuters, 14 July 2022; Council on Foreign Relations, 'Oil dependence and U.S. foreign policy 1850–2023', www.cfr.org.
14 Section 101(b), *Consolidated Appropriations Act 2016*, signed into law on 18 December 2015.
15 Yoshi Tsurumi, 'The oil crisis: In perspective', *Daedalus*, vol. 104, no. 4, 1975, 113–27.
16 Bruce Cumings, *The Origins of the Korean War, Vol. II*, Princeton University Press, 1990, 56–7.
17 US Energy Information Administration, 'Country analysis brief: Japan', 7 July 2023.
18 *New York Times*, 'Fahd said to deny causing oil chaos in talks with Bush', 7 April 1986.

19 George Bush Presidential Library and Museum, 'National Security Strategy report, March 1990', 13.

20 Zbigniew Brzezinski, 'Hegemonic quicksand', *The National Interest*, 1 December 2003.

21 US Department of the Treasury, 'Major Foreign Holders of Treasury Securities'.

22 Noam Chomsky in conversation with Ira Shorr, *America's Defense Monitor* and the Center for Defence Information, 11 February 1996.

23 Natalie Andrews and Alexander Ward, 'Trump plans to visit Saudi Arabia, Qatar in first foreign trip', *Wall Street Journal*, 31 March 2025.

24 Christopher Blanchard, 'Qatar: Issues for the 119th Congress', Congressional Research Service, 13 May 2025.

25 Frederic Lane, *Venice and History*, Johns Hopkins Press, 1966, 373–428. For an in-depth explanation of 'protection costs', see 389–90, 416–20.

26 Stefan Kanfer, *Somebody: The Reckless Life and Remarkable Career of Marlon Brando*, Alfred A Knopf, 2008, 114. See also Alfred W McCoy, *The Politics of Heroin: C.I.A. Complicity in the Global Drug Trade*, Lawrence Hill Books, 2003, 461–93.

27 Javier Blas, 'Never mind those EVs – Oil demand keeps growing', Bloomberg, 13 May 2024.

28 Jeremy Sharp, 'US foreign aid to Israel', Congressional Research Service, 1 March 2023.

29 Ibid.

30 This section relies on Philip Dorling, *The Origins of the ANZUS Treaty: A Reconsideration*, Flinders University, 1989.

31 John Mueller and Karl Mueller, 'Sanctions of mass destruction', *Foreign Affairs*, vol. 78, no. 3, May–June 1999.

32 Professor Anuradha Chenoy, 'Gender and human rights violations as structural part of unilateral coercive measures', Seminar of Experts on Unilateral Coercive Measures, Human Rights Council, United Nations, Geneva, 5 April 2013.

33 Ted Clark and Renee Montagne, 'UN official protests Iraqi sanctions', NPR News Morning Edition, 8 October 1998.
34 Wael Faleh, 'Former UN officers say "genocidal" Iraqi embargo must end', Associated Press, 18 June 2001.
35 Richard Garfield, 'Morbidity and mortality among Iraqi children from 1990 through 1998: Assessing the impact of the Gulf War and economic sanctions', Relief Web, 30 March 1999.
36 Richard Marles, interview with Patricia Karvelas, 'Government deploys "contingency" troops to Middle East', ABC Radio National Breakfast, 25 October 2023 at 7am.
37 Jordyn Beazley, Royce Kurmelovs and Amy Remeikis, 'Thousands gather for pro-Palestine rallies', *Guardian*, 16 October 2023.
38 Department of Foreign Affairs and Trade, 'Joint statement on Australia–U.S. ministerial consultations 2022', 6 December 2022.
39 UNODC, *Prison Matters 2024: Global Prison Population and Trends; A Focus on Rehabilitation*, United Nations, 2024, 12.
40 Human Rights Watch, 'A threshold crossed: Israeli authorities and the crimes of apartheid and persecution', April 2021; Amnesty International, 'Israel's apartheid against Palestinians: Cruel system of domination and crime against humanity', February 2022; B'Tselem – The Israeli Information Center for Human Rights in the Occupied Territories, 'A regime of Jewish supremacy from the Jordan River to the Mediterranean Sea: This is apartheid', January 2021.
41 Independent International Commission of Inquiry on the Occupied Palestinian Territory, including East Jerusalem, and Israel, '"More than a human can bear": Israel's systematic use of sexual, reproductive and other forms of gender-based violence since 7 October 2023', Human Rights Council, 58th session, 13 March 2025.
42 Ibid.
43 Hans M Kristensen and Matt Korda, 'Israeli nuclear weapons, 2021', *Bulletin of the Atomic Scientists*, vol. 78, no. 1, 2022, 38–50; Philip Dorling, 'Australia still denies Israel's open secret of a nuclear arsenal', *The Age*, 15 April 2014.
44 Dorling, 'Australia still denies Israel's open secret'.

45 Steve Weissman and Herbert Krosney, *The Islamic Bomb: The Nuclear Threat to Israel and the Middle East*, Times Books, 1981, 114–17.
46 104th Congress, *National Defense Authorization Act 1997*, Sec. 1064, 'Prohibition on collection and release of detailed satellite imagery relating to Israel', 30 July 1996.
47 Hans M Kristensen and Matt Korda, 'Nuclear Notebook: Israeli nuclear weapons, 2022', *Bulletin of the Atomic Scientists*, 17 January 2022.
48 Avner Cohen, *Israel Crosses the Threshold,* National Security Archive Electronic Briefing Book No. 189, 28 April 2006; National Security Archive, Memorandum, 'Henry Owen to the Secretary, "Impact on U.S. policies of an Israeli nuclear weapons capability"', 7 February 1969.
49 Adam Entous, 'How Trump and three other US presidents protected Israel's worst-kept secret: Its nuclear arsenal', *New Yorker*, 18 June 2018.
50 Natasha Bertrand and Alex Marquardt, 'Leaked documents show US intelligence on Israel's plans to attack Iran, sources say', CNN, 20 October 2024.
51 Stephen Bryen, 'US intel leak shakes Israel's plan to hit Iran, and more', *Asia Times*, 21 October 2024.
52 Kristensen and Korda, 'Israeli nuclear weapons, 2021'.
53 William Burr and Avner Cohen (eds), *Israel Crosses the Threshold II*, National Security Archive Electronic Briefing Book No. 485, 12 September 2014.
54 Perry Stein and Michael Birnbaum, 'FBI investigates alleged leak of U.S. insights on Israeli war preparation', *Washington Post*, 22 October 2024.
55 Kristensen and Korda, 'Israeli nuclear weapons, 2021'.
56 Penny Wong, 'Sanctions in response to Iran's nuclear and missile programs', media release, 18 October 2023.
57 Nuno Luzio, 'The IAEA and a nuclear-weapon-free zone in the Middle East', *IAEA Bulletin*, vol. 62-4, December 2021.

58 Wong, 'Sanctions in response to Iran's nuclear and missile programs'.
59 UN Security Council Resolution 687 (1991), 8 April 1991.
60 WikiLeaks, US State Department, 2008 Annual Intelligence and Research – Office of National Assessments intelligence exchange, 17 November 2008.
61 Lieutenant General Robert Ashley (Director, US Defense Intelligence Agency), 'Statement for the record: Worldwide Threat Assessment 2018', 6 March 2018.
62 Lieutenant General Ronald L Burgess (Director, US Defense Intelligence Agency), 'Statement before the Committee on Armed Services', US Senate, 14 April 2010.
63 Ibid.
64 Kelsey Davenport, Daryl G Kimball and Greg Thielmann, *Solving the Iranian Nuclear Puzzle: The Joint Comprehensive Plan of Action*, Arms Control Association, August 2015, 47.
65 Adam Taylor and Meg Kelly, 'Iran's missile attack on Israel raises questions about limits of arsenal', *Washington Post*, 5 October 2024.
66 Office of the Historian, *Foreign Relations of the United States, 1958–1960, Volume XIV: Africa,* Document 336, Telegram from the Embassy in South Africa to the Department of State (7 November 1958), US Department of State, 1992.
67 Shira Rubin and Ellen Nakashima, 'Netanyahu tells U.S. that Israel will strike Iranian military, not nuclear or oil, targets, officials say', *Washington Post*, 15 October 2024.
68 Antony Loewenstein, *The Palestine Laboratory: How Israel Exports the Technology of Occupation around the World*, Verso, 2023, 90, 137, 143–9, 155–6.

4 FRONTLINE CHINA

1 Andrew Greene, 'Australian helicopter forced to take evasive action after Chinese fighter detonates flares', ABC News, 6 May 2025.

2 Alex Horton and Hannah Natanson, 'Secret Pentagon memo on China, homeland has Heritage fingerprints', *Washington Post*, 29 March 2025.
3 Royal Australian Navy, Capabilities, 'HMAS Hobart (III)', www.navy.gov.au.
4 Robert M Clark, *The Technical Collection of Intelligence*, CQ Press, 2010, 221–7.
5 Robert S Norris and Hans M Kristensen, 'U.S. nuclear threats: Then and now', *Bulletin of the Atomic Scientists*, vol. 62, no. 5, 2006, 69–71.
6 Barton Bernstein, 'The perils and politics of surrender: Ending the war with Japan and avoiding the third atomic bomb', *Pacific Historical Review*, vol. 46, no. 1, 1977, 1–27.
7 Ward Wilson, *Five Myths about Nuclear Weapons*, Mariner Books, 2014.
8 Harry Truman, The President's News Conference, 30 November 1950, Harry S Truman Library.
9 David McCullough, *Truman*, Simon & Schuster 1993, 822.
10 Norris and Kristensen, 'U.S. nuclear threats: Then and now', 69–71.
11 Andrew Nathan and Andrew Scobell, *China's Search for Security*, Columbia University Press, 2012, 17.
12 Tong Zhao, *Tides of Change: China's Nuclear Ballistic Missile Submarines and Strategic Stability*, Carnegie Endowment for International Peace, 2018, 14.
13 US Department of Defense, 'Military and security developments involving the People's Republic of China', Annual Report to Congress, 2023, 55; Annual Report to Congress, 2024, 53, 56, 88, 104; Hans M Kristensen, Matt Korda, Eliana Johns and Mackenzie Knight, 'Chinese nuclear weapons, 2025', *Bulletin of the Atomic Scientists*, vol. 81 no. 2, 135–60.
14 Defense Intelligence Ballistic Missile Analysis Committee, *2020 Ballistic and Cruise Missile Threat*, National Air and Space Intelligence Center, July 2020.

15 Defense Technical Information Center, *The People's Liberation Army Navy: A Modern Navy with Chinese Characteristics*, Office of Naval Intelligence, 2009.
16 Wu Riqiang, 'Survivability of China's sea-based nuclear forces', *Science & Global Security*, vol. 19, no. 2, 2011.
17 Henry Foy, Polina Ivanova, Kathrin Hille and Demetri Sevastopulos, 'US accuses China of directly supporting Russia's "war machine"', *Financial Times*, 11 September 2024.
18 Tom Stefanick, *Strategic Antisubmarine Warfare and Naval Strategy*, Lexington Books, 1987, 265–71; Owen R Cote Jr, *The Third Battle: Innovation in the U.S. Navy's Silent Cold War Struggle with Soviet Submarines*, Naval War College Newport Papers No. 16, Naval War College Press, 2003, 22–3.
19 Brendan Rittenhouse Green and Caitlin Talmadge, 'Then what? Assessing the military implications of Chinese control of Taiwan', *International Security*, vol. 47, no. 1, 2022, 7–45.
20 Jian Lan, Ningning Zhang, and Yu Wang, 'On the dynamics of the South China Sea deep circulation', *Journal of Geophysical Research: Oceans*, vol. 118, 1206–10.
21 Justin Burke, 'The cause for China's coercion in the skies may lay under the water', Lowy Institute, 13 May 2024.
22 Kirsten Sellars, *A 'Constitution for the Oceans': The Long Hard Road to the UN Convention on the Law of the Sea*, Cambridge University Press, 2025.
23 Isaac Kardon, *China's Law of the Sea*, Yale University Press, 2023, 197.
24 Ben Blanchard, 'Freedom of navigation patrols may end "in disaster"' – Chinese admiral', Reuters, 19 July 2016.
25 Oriana Skylar Mastro, 'How China is bending the rules in the South China Sea', Lowy Institute, 17 February 2021.
26 Robert E Johannes and JW MacFarlane, *Traditional Fishing in the Torres Strait Islands*, CSIRO Fisheries Division, 1991.
27 Philip Dorling, 'Reef safeguard cut back', *The Age*, 12 September 2011.

28 WikiLeaks, 'Torres Strait pilotage regime', 08CANBERRA773_a, 31 July 2008.
29 International Maritime Organisation, Marine Environment Protection Committee, 49th session, Agenda Item 8, MEPC 49/8, Extension of Existing Great Barrier Reef PSSA to include the Torres Strait Region submitted by Australia and Papua New Guinea, 10 April 2003. I thank Andrew Serdy for his insights.
30 Australian Maritime Safety Authority, Marine Notice 7/2009, 17 April 2009.
31 Dorling, 'Reef safeguard cut back'.
32 Keir Lieber and Daryl Press, *The Myth of the Nuclear Revolution*, Cornell University Press, 2020.
33 Keir Lieber and Daryl Press, 'The new era of counterforce: Technological change and the future of nuclear deterrence', *International Security*, vol. 41, no. 4, 2017, 9–49.
34 ABC News (Australia), 'Panmunjom Declaration for Peace, Prosperity and Unification of the Korean Peninsula', 27 April 2018.
35 Josh Smith and Phil Stewart, 'Trump surprises with pledge to end military exercises in South Korea', Reuters, 13 June 2018; Reuters, 'Trump says to stop "expensive", "provocative" South Korea war games', 12 June 2018.
36 Connor O'Brien and Jacqueline Feldscher, 'Pelosi asks Joint Chiefs about preventing Trump from launching nukes', *Politico*, 8 January 2021.
37 Elizabeth N Saunders, 'There is no legal way to stop Trump from ordering a nuclear strike if he wants to, expert says', *Washington Post*, 9 January 2021.
38 Jon Letman, 'Trump just inherited sole authority to launch nuclear weapons on a whim', *Truthout*, 20 January 2025.
39 US Strategic Command, Policy Committee, 'Essentials of post-Cold War deterrence', 1995, obtained under the *Freedom of Information Act* by Hans M Kristensen, available at the Nuclear Information Project, www.nukestrat.com.

40 Douglas MacArthur, 'Memorandum on Formosa, 14 June 1950', Office of the Historian, *Foreign Relations of the United States 1950, Volume VII: Korea*, US Department of State, 1976.
41 Douglas MacArthur, 'Address to Congress', 19 April 1951, Library of Congress.
42 E Ratner, 'Statement before the United States Senate Committee on Foreign Relations', 8 December 2021.
43 Luke Gosling, 'Deterring at a distance: The strategic logic of AUKUS', Lowy Institute, 24 June 2024.

5 DEMONSTRATING RELEVANCE: THE STRATEGIC LOGIC OF AUKUS

1 Australian Submarine Agency, 'Further boost to Australia's nuclear-powered submarine workforce', media release, 3 September 2024. The individuals were Richard Marles, Pat Conroy and Andrew Hastie, but they are basically interchangeable with anyone else in those portfolios. I have italicised '*nation-building*' throughout for emphasis.
2 Andrew Hastie, 'AUKUS is a "nation-building task" that will span generations', interview with Kieran Gilbert, Sky News Australia, 19 March 2023.
3 Matthew Knott, 'Ignore the AUKUS hand-wringers, we need these subs for sea-bed battles: Navy chief', *Sydney Morning Herald*, 15 April 2023.
4 Defence Department, Australian Submarine Agency 2023, Corporate Plan 2023–27, 8; Richard Marles and Pat Conroy, joint media release, 'Launch of the Australian Submarine Agency', 1 July 2023. See also his opening statement at Senate Budget Estimates, 6 June 2024.
5 Nuclear Threat Initiative, 'South Korea submarine capabilities', 20 August 2024.
6 Doug Thomas, 'Air-Independent Propulsion submarines', *Canadian Naval Review*, vol. 3, no. 4, Winter 2008.

7 Nuclear Threat Initiative, 'Germany submarine capabilities', 28 August 2024.
8 Janes Database, 'Spanish S-80 submarine programme hits new milestones while Navantia pursues export opportunities', accessed 21 March 2025.
9 Nuclear Threat Initiative, 'Italy submarine capabilities', 21 August 2024.
10 Peter Roberts, 'Patrick releases defence shopping list to replace N-subs', Australian Manufacturing Forum, 18 July 2022.
11 Alan Kuperman, 'The US Navy's nuclear proliferation problem', *Breaking Defense*, 15 September 2021.
12 Article IV (B) of AUKUS.
13 International Atomic Energy Agency, 'Information Circular', Article 14.
14 Article VII (F) of AUKUS.
15 For further discussion, see Ambassador Ian Biggs, Head of Delegation and Resident Representative of Australia to the IAEA, AUKUS Trilateral Right of Reply – Item 21: Transfer of the nuclear materials in the context of AUKUS and its safeguards in all aspects under the NPT, 19 September 2024.
16 Philip Dorling, 'Albo and the nukes – the demise of Labor's disarmament policy', MichaelWestMedia, 12 May 2023.
17 Rex Patrick and Philip Dorling, 'Nuke policy quietly nuked: Australia to fund US nuclear weapon delivery program', Michael WestMedia, 2 January 2024.
18 Anya L Fink, 'Nuclear-Armed Sea-Launched Cruise Missile (SLCM-N)', Congressional Research Service, 12 February 2025.
19 Senate Foreign Affairs, Defence and Trade Committee Estimates, *Hansard,* 88–89, 6 June 2024.
20 Australian Submarine Agency 2023, Corporate Plan 2023–27, 8. Richard Marles and Pat Conroy, joint media release, 'Launch of the Australian Submarine Agency', 1 July 2023. See also his opening statement at Senate Budget Estimates, 6 June 2024.

21 Ronald O'Rourke, 'Navy Virginia-Class Submarine Program and AUKUS Submarine (Pillar 1) Project: Background and issues for Congress', Library of Congress, 10 October 2024.
22 Andrew Fowler, *Nuked: The Submarine Fiasco that Sank Australia's Sovereignty*, Melbourne University Publishing, 2024.
23 Michael Miller, 'With Trump's win, Australia worries AUKUS may come under new scrutiny', *Washington Post*, 8 November 2024.
24 John Blaxland, 'A second suitable piece of real estate', Lowy Institute, 17 July 2024.
25 James Mulvenon, 'Chairman Hu and the PLA's "New Historic Missions"', *China Leadership Monitor*, no. 27, Winter, 2009.
26 Michael Miller, 'Australia offers U.S. a vast new military launchpad in China conflict', *Washington Post*, 24 August 2024.
27 Stephen Smith and Angus Houston, *Defence Strategic Review*, 2023, 77.
28 Rex Patrick, 'Fuel security! What fuel security? A government security blunder', MichaelWestMedia, 2 May 2023.
29 Malcolm Sutton, 'Australia's fuel security falling short as "war-game" report, released under FOI, reveals vulnerabilities', ABC, 7 January 2025.
30 Department of Climate Change, Energy, the Environment and Water, *Australian Energy Update 2024*, August 2024, 20.
31 Ashley Townshend, 'The AUKUS submarine deal highlights a tectonic shift in the US–Australia alliance', Carnegie Endowment Commentary, 27 March 2023.
32 Damien Cave, 'Why more American weapons will soon be made outside America', *New York Times*, 1 March 2024.
33 US Department of State, Joint Statement on AUSMIN, 6 August 2024.
34 John Tirpak, 'Three B-2 bombers land in Australia', *Air and Space Forces Magazine*, 19 August 2024.
35 Eric Heginbotham, *U.S.–China Military Scorecard 1996–2017*, RAND Corporation, 2015.

36 Zuri Linetsky, 'America's Marines prepare for an unwanted pacific war with China', *Foreign Policy*, 16 September 2024.
37 Jason Koutsoukis, 'Pezzullo: Labor has "picked a side" in war with China', *Saturday Paper*, 31 August 2024.
38 Australian Space Agency, Expert Reference Group, *Review of Australia's Space Industry Capability*, 1 March 2018, 20.
39 Elbridge Colby, 'Against the Great Powers: Reflections on balancing nuclear and conventional power', *Texas National Security Review*, vol. 2, no. 1, November 2018, 152.
40 Office of the Historian, *Foreign Relations of the United States, 1952–1954, Volume II, Part 1: National Security Affairs*, Memorandum by the Director of the Policy Planning Staff (Nitze) to the Deputy Under Secretary of State (Matthews) (14 July 1952), US Department of State, 1984.
41 Lewis Frederickson, 'The development of Australian infantry on the Western Front 1916–1918: An imperial model of training, tactics and technology', PhD thesis, UNSW Canberra, 2015, 135.
42 Joseph Cook, 29 November 1909, in Peter Dennis, et al. (eds), *The Oxford Companion to Australian Military History*, Oxford, 1995, 517.
43 Clinton Fernandes, *Subimperial Power*, Melbourne University Publishing, 2022, 32–58.

6 TURBULENCE

1 Albert Palazzo, *The Big Fix: Rebuilding Australia's National Security*, Melbourne University Publishing, 2025.
2 Glenn Frey, Don Felder and Don Henley, 'Hotel California', Asylum Records, 8 December 1976.
3 The White House, 'Fact sheet: President Donald J. Trump restores Section 232 tariffs', 11 February 2025.
4 Roger Geiger, *Research and Relevant Knowledge: American Research Universities Since World War II*, Oxford University Press, 1993, 30–197.

5 Michel Crozier, Samuel P Huntington and Joji Watanuki, *Crisis of Democracy: Report on the Governability of Democracies to the Trilateral Commission*, New York University Press, 1975; Noam Chomsky, Richard Lewontin and Ira Katznelson, *The Cold War and the University: Toward an Intellectual History of the Postwar Years*, The New Press, 1998.

6 Ralph W Emerson, 'Circles' (1841), *The Complete Essays and other Writings*, Modern Library, 1950, 288.

7 Graham Fuller, 'In great power diplomacy, is China beating US at its own game?', *Responsible Statecraft*, 13 March 2023.

8 'US remains the best place to invest overseas, says AustralianSuper's CIO', *Financial Times Europe*, 11 April 2025.

9 Clinton Fernandes, *Subimperial Power*, Melbourne University Publishing, 2022.

10 Douglas MacArthur, 'Address to Congress', 19 April 1951.

11 Ben McKelvey, *Find Fix Finish*, HarperCollins, 2022, 224.

12 Ben Feller and Julie Pace, 'Obama's Afghanistan plan criticized on two fronts', NBC News, 23 June 2011; Simon Tisdall, 'Obama U-turn on troops withdrawal makes Afghanistan an election issue', *Guardian*, 16 October 2015.

13 Rafael Epstein, 'The secret soldiers', *Sydney Morning Herald*, 5 September 2011.

14 Evan A Feigenbaum, 'Asia's future beyond U.S.–China competition', Carnegie Endowment for International Peace, 9 September 2020.

15 UN Population Fund, 'Adolescents and youth in the Arab States region', arabstates.unfpa.org.

16 Liz Sly, 'Lost decade: The unfinished business of the Arab spring', *Washington Post*, 24 January 2021.

17 Ruth First, *The Barrel of a Gun: Political Power in Africa and the Coup d'Etat*, Penguin, 1970.

18 Zleekhah Mohtaseb, in discussion with Senator Nick Xenophon (Independent, South Australia), Hebron (al-Khalil), 7 May 2014.

19 James Jupp, *The English in Australia*, Cambridge University Press, 2004, 1; Keith Willey, 'Australia's population', *Labour History*, vol. 35, no. 1, 1978, 1–9.
20 Clinton Fernandes, 'Remembering US-funded state terror in Central America', *Crikey*, 22 November 2019.
21 Connie Levett, 'Police urged to arrest East Timor collaborator', *The Age*, 26 September 2008.

INDEX